SCIENCE AND CULTURE SERIES
JOSEPH HUSSLEIN, S.J., Ph.D., GENERAL EDITOR

CHURCH ARCHITECTURE:
BUILDING FOR A LIVING FAITH

CHURCH ARCHITECTURE

Building for a LIVING FAITH

By FRANK BRANNACH

MEMBER OF THE FEDERATION OF CATHOLIC ART
AND THE LITURGICAL ARTS SOCIETY

THE BRUCE PUBLISHING COMPANY
MILWAUKEE

Nihil obstat:
 H. B. RIES,
  Censor librorum

Imprimatur:
 ✠ SAMUEL A. STRITCH,
  Archiepiscopus Milwaukiensis

September 7, 1932

Art is nothing else than right reason in the doing of work; the excellence of which consists not in appealing to others but in being good in itself. — Saint Thomas Aquinas, in *Summa Theologica,* Question LVII, Article III.

"What is the highest of the arts? Each art will answer that question by a claim to the superiority for itself. I shall answer it by saying that the art which does most to develop all the arts is the highest. Architecture is that art. Architecture is the Pantheon of all the arts. Under the roof of its own masterpieces that lift its message above the earth, it shelters the works it inspires. Sculpture carves its arches and fills its niches, fashions its solid adornment within and without. Painting beautifies its altars and brightens its shrines. Ceramics calls the glory of the sun through the painted glass to fill its dim spaces with magic colors. Music rolls melody through its pillared cloisters. No art that appeals to the soul is a stranger in the palace of architecture, from the tapestry that hangs over a balcony to the chased chalice upon the altar. Architecture alone can make such a sweeping claim to leadership. The Ten Christian Centuries recognized this and gave us the glory of architecture, not in the heavy but beautiful horizontal and vertical lines of the worldly Greek, but in the curves of the Roman and Gothic that suggest the rainbow starting its brilliant upward climb from two points on earth and meeting in a blaze of beauty high in the heavens. Christian architecture is Christian thought. It animates the dumb stone, bids it preach and teach, organizes and spiritualizes matter to give it a soul of its own, and joins all the arts and all the inert materials with which they work in a psalm without words which God hears as another *Benedictus*. It is only the world of Christ that could produce such a triumph."

—*The Forgotten God,* Most Reverend Francis Clement Kelley, Bishop of Oklahoma City.

PREFACE BY THE GENERAL EDITOR

At no time perhaps has the need of a volume on church architecture been more evident than at the present moment. The demand for literature in this field is growing apace. Help and direction are eagerly sought. The spread of education, too, calls for an intelligent understanding of this subject. We are witnessing, in fact, the dawn of a new era in church architecture.

In secular architecture great changes have already taken place. Babylonic structures, mounting stage on stage, are rapidly transforming the skylines of our cities. But the canons of artistic treatment are not for this reason forgotten. Titanic vastness is not seldom combined with stately grandeur; baffling height is matched with well-planned beauty of proportion. We have passed through the crude beginnings of the skyscraper period, and years ago was erected the first Gothic tower of commerce, which proved to be an architectural achievement, the Woolworth Building in New York City.

True, it is an age of concrete, steel, and terra cotta. But why assume that these materials, when honestly used, do not present artistic possibilities as fully legitimate as wood or stone? Nor are the latter disregarded in the new art and architecture.

Here, then, is the problem confronting in our day the church architect. He must bring forth from his treasury, where study and observation have stored them, *nova et vetera,* "things new and old." But what is most important, his imagination, guided by a true judgment, must know how to combine, for best effect, the new with the old, the modern with the traditional, whether in structure or in ornament.

Nor may clergy and people be less concerned with these developments. Once more they should learn to express, as far as possible today, a corporate interest such as was displayed by the entire populations of the little towns during the Ages of Faith when there arose, over all of Europe, the marvelous cathedrals which still remain the architectural wonder of the world.

Our churches, it is true, will generally be less stupendous and magnificent in their proportions. Yet the same conscientious care should be taken in lovingly designing the smallest chapel as in elaborately planning the largest cathedral. But properly to perform this task, priests and people must acquire at least some fundamental knowledge of the subject here discussed. They should have some understanding of historic styles, in structure and in decoration. To this should be added an appreciation of the manner in which Christian traditions of bygone generations can be correctly adapted to modern uses, new materials, and progressive inventions.

To make easily accessible to all the opportunity of acquiring this knowledge, the present volume has been prepared, and is here offered, in the Science and Culture Series, as an original and highly practical contribution. By means of combined text and illustration it brings home the basic lessons which every intelligent reader should learn to understand.

Such, then, has been the aim of the author in this greatly needed work, which appears at the strategic moment when the history of modern church architecture is as yet not so much to be written as to be made. His book should help to point out the path and lead in the right direction.

The author's purpose, as already intimated, was not to reject in any way the long experience and the rich tradition of the past, but prudently to suggest the adaptation of them to present needs and opportunities. Thus will be avoided the servile and often impracticable imitation of famous works of other ages, while the way is laid open for the creation of a distinctively new and great Christian church architecture, *modern yet not modernistic,* inheriting all that is best in the past, yet leaving untrammeled freedom for every legitimate initiative.

The ancient Egyptian builders, massing huge slabs of stone over seried rows of ponderous pillars, each with its carved lotus capital; or basing on immovable rock the broad foundation of his polished pyramid, with its dead blocks piled up in mathematical precision and destined to inclose the mortal remains of a deified Pharaoh, was at all events working honestly in his material and expressing correctly, to the best of his power, a materialistic creed, which was not without its spiritual significance.

The Greek architect, gifted with a delicate perception of purely physical beauty, and with unprecedented perfection in his sense of proportion, carried to marvelous attainment that symmetry of structure and charm of natural form which no other nation has ever surpassed. He, too, worked true to his ideals and faithfully expressed the spirit of his race, with its naturalistic bent and its visions of Olympian deities feasting in mansions of burnished bronze and little recking of human needs.

At length came the Christian artist. Confined at first to a purely subterranean art, he decorated with symbolic designs the vaults of his catacombs. Emerging, next, into the light of day, he found himself welcomed into imperial halls, where the Divine Mysteries were celebrated. Imitating, in turn, with wise adaptations, the regal structures and civic halls of justice, he produced a style rightly termed Basilican. Everywhere the material for this form of building was on hand. The very slabs and pillars of earlier edifices might be incorporated into his own, until more original structures could be erected, not unworthy of the King of kings. So arose the world's famous basilicas, which remain to the present day among the supreme achievements in Christian church architecture.

Other styles were now to follow, as the centuries passed, until among the Franco-German people we find at last a clear though primitive development of what in future ages was to receive the name "Gothic."

How precisely the first impetus was given in Christian Europe to this new style may be difficult to determine with any certainty. Its evolution was strictly the work of Christian builders, though something may well have been contributed by the recollections of Oriental structures — visions of filmy beauty, of arches artistically broken — that lingered on in the memories of the early crusaders as, with shields slung over their shoulders, they returned, after hard-fought battles and perilous campaigns, to their homes in the West. Particularly rich in suggestion, at all events, may have been the Syrian marches of the crusading hosts.

Yet, if so, they did not blindly copy the things they had seen, when chisel and trowel replaced in their hand the sword and spear. Little importance is today attached to the influence of the Crusades on Gothic architecture. Yet, whenceever the ideas may have been derived, at a period preceding all these events, the men of those ages adapted, with skillful art, the new to the old, invented processes all their own, and evolved the consummation of a style that flowered forth in those marvels of majesty and beauty that still remain the wonder and despair of our modern world, the great medieval Gothic cathedrals. But best of all, it was a style typically Catholic — strong, graceful, lofty — embracing the finest traditions of the Christian past and expressing, as never before, the spirituality of the Catholic Faith.

Soaring upward, its sweeping lines of arch and vault sprang from leaf-crowned pillars, while its high walls were pierced with mullioned windows and sustained by buttresses artistically placed. Within, speaking to the heart of these lovers of nature and nature's God, were gently mingled the lights and shadows of their ancient forests, clinging softly around oaklike rows of massive pillars and underneath the vaulted archings as of woodland boughs, while in the air about them hung the roseate tints of dawn and the hues of all the flowers, blended as the light of morning fell through richly stained and storied windows, at the Sacring of the Mass. It was a vision of earth and heaven, a full recognition of all the needs of human nature and at the same time a lifting up of the spiritual soul, and with it of man's entire being to the worship of his Creator.

And all day long, wherever the gildsman toiled, his thoughts might, without any effort, mount to God as he gazed upon the wondrous structure which his own hands had helped to raise, while his eyes followed upward, with keen delight, through the misty haze of thronging spires, until his spirit, too, was caught up and swept along, as on strong eagle wings, with the mighty soaring of the giant steeple. But without halting there, his heart could pierce still further, into the blue beyond, and his soul might dream of the Celestial Vision.

That, and no less than that, is what we mean when we speak of the spiritual quality of the Gothic. And here, no doubt, it will be of interest to recall a statement confidently made years ago by that esthetic Catholic poet and essayist, Coventry Patmore, whose views on architecture are not likely to be familiar to many at the present day.

His assertion was that three styles only were possible, and that these three had already been invented. They were: the Egyptian, the Greek, and the Gothic. The first of these expressed perfectly the material element; the second, the rational; and the third, the spiritual. Nothing further remained for architecture to say. The cycle was closed. Other so-called styles could come into existence, but they would be only blendings, modifications, or variations of the three fundamental types.

Whatever our own reactions may be to such a statement, it brings home to us in a startling manner the underlying thought that all true architecture is an authentic expression. Hence, whatever styles there are — and let us count as many as we may —

[xi]

each is the specific expression of the ideals, aspirations, and characteristics of the men who planned it and developed it. Adopted by the people of other times and other climes, it must not merely be adapted to new materials and new surroundings, but must be made to convey in some degree at least an expression of the new civilization and new outlook upon life of those who use it.

If our own architectural contributions have been paltry in the past, there is better hope for the future. The rifts in the clouds have been widening and we catch golden glimpses of the breaking day beyond, in ecclesiastical as well as in secular architecture. The illustrations in the present book will themselves help to make this visible.

The author, I should explain, is a Catholic priest, writing under the pen name of Frank Brannach. For fifteen years he has contributed articles on church architecture to the Catholic press. Previous to that, during a prolonged residence in Europe, he familiarized himself with the masterpieces of both pagan and Christian art and architecture, thus laying the foundation for his work. Though rightly progressive in his views, he is in no sense a modernist. While he would stimulate a creative spirit in our Christian church architecture, he would do so, not by rejecting the rich heritage of past Christian centuries, but by urging men to utilize it to the utmost, without loss of their own originality, that they, too, may contribute in turn what their own age has to give. So did the great styles of the past come into being. Rigid logic and honesty of work are insisted upon by him, that we may produce an architecture worthy of our Faith.

Such, fundamentally, are the author's views, who here addresses himself to a wide range of readers: to students and masters in the field; to architects, decorators, and furnishers; but in particular to the clergy and the laity. Great improvement in church building, he believes, cannot be hoped for until the parishioners themselves have learned to value the beauty of God's house. For years he has sought to reach the latter through the pages of the Catholic Art Bulletin in the *Catholic Daily Tribune,* while he has approached the clergy through a series of articles in the *Acolyte.* The present volume should carry his message to still wider circles of readers.

And here the Editor may make free to state that all due attention has been gladly given by him to this volume, whose subject is one that has ever been close to his own heart, as it should be close to the heart of every Christian man and woman — church architecture.

> Joseph Husslein, S.J., Ph.D.,
> *General Editor, Science and Culture Series.*

St. Louis University,
February 24, 1932.

FOREWORD

For four hundred years pagan humanism has ruled the world in its destructive power. This has led in government to national rivalry; in religion to indifference; in art to affectation ending recently in mathematical ugliness. Life was destined to be hopeless and art grotesque.

The practical logic of life has come to ultimate conclusions. We cannot go on as before. It is time for a change. If humanism does not work, it should be rejected. If Christianity alone can make life more beautiful and more spiritual, we may conclude that it is lasting as truth and should be tried as never before in modern times.

Those who think man is no more than a stone — an aimless creature gathering a little moss and then disintegrating — build of stone without ornament, a pile of material treasure. But those who know that man cannot be symbolized by soulless fate-driven rocks build indeed of stone but they add something to it. To represent the fullness of life it must be beautified and blessed.

But for the religious spirit we need not go back to ancient times, admirable though they be. The Church is interested in her glorious yesterday but brings God's grace to men today and tomorrow. She does not abandon a soul after the sacrament of regeneration but is interested in its welfare until it appears for judgment. So it is unreasonable to say that religious inspiration in church building ended with the thirteenth century. It will end only with the "consummation of the world."

Great churches have been built in the past in many various styles, but we must make our contribution and interpret the Church to the present age. Borrowing Gothic forms from the past, or Romanesque or Renaissance modes of expression, means nothing to the living present. Old forms are not even interesting.

[xv]

FOREWORD

Until recently many of the churches in this country were gloomy and hopeless as the age which they represented. Many of them were costly, but marble walls and gold vessels do not always represent religion. Sometimes they mean only wealth — wasted wealth.

The Church has a message for a materialistic age. Religion ennobles life and brings happiness. It teaches industrialism the virtue of charity and the inspiration of beauty. For spirituality there can be no depression, as hope always endures. Materialism, hatred, and ugliness have failed. It is time now to return to faith, charity, and beauty.

One of the signs of the times is the rebuilding, in England, of Buckfast Abbey by Benedictine monks, knowing as they did that loving devotion cannot be hired for a wage.

The illustrations in this volume show a growing improvement in the American contribution of originality and artistic effort in the beautification of the House of God. We are less interested now in conventional prettiness than in honest material and suitability to purpose. We find more beauty in the vigor of rough granite than in the over-refinement of polished marble.

Some of the ideas expressed here were printed elsewhere in criticism and protest, but in recognition of the many splendid churches recently erected the tone has been changed to one of praise. The author has been encouraged to continue by the acceptance without comment of what he has previously written as based on truth and right reason. May this new effort add to the "greater glory of God"!

FRANK BRANNACH

CONTENTS

[xvii]

CONTENTS

LIST OF ILLUSTRATIONS

LIST OF ILLUSTRATIONS

LIST OF ILLUSTRATIONS

Chapter I

LITURGY AND BEAUTY

LITURGY is the public worship of God by His Church. From Apostolic times it has made use of the beauty of painting and song to give honor to God and to promote the devotion of His people. Even in the sad days of the Roman persecutions, when the hounded Christians were forced to take to the underground cemeteries for refuge, the rough-hewn walls of volcanic ashes were coated with lime plaster and painted with the symbols of faith and worship. When peace came with the edict of Constantine in 313, that magnanimous ruler set an example to the world for all future time in building Christian temples of such beauty and solidity that they remain down to our own day as a testimonial of faith. When Constantinople was made his capital, that city became the center of religious art and remained so for a thousand years. The West was almost abandoned, but even there efforts were made to preserve the beauty of God's house. The Empress Galla Placidia and the Emperor Theodoric caused admirable churches to be erected in Ravenna, the Western capital.

Very few churches built between the sixth and tenth centuries have been preserved for us. The edifices then erected may have been destroyed, but probably the time itself was little favorable for building. Such churches, however, as do remain are works of art. Great skill, too, was then displayed in the illuminating of manuscripts by monks and nuns, while metal, enamel, and ivory workers showed genuine appreciation of beauty. In northern Italy a number of noteworthy churches have come down to us from that time.

Many centuries elapsed before paganism entirely disappeared. But a new civilization then began to develop. Instead of criticizing the Dark Ages we should rather admire them for their

[1]

10268

struggle toward the light. The ruins of Roman temples and theaters became an inspiration for the building of beautiful and substantial churches in what was later called the Romanesque style. If the buildings were crude they were nevertheless devotional.

Then came the Gothic age, the age of the Crusades and of great scholars and saints. The beauty and majesty of the Gothic cathedrals built at that period have not been surpassed by man in any age. They might be rivaled only by the temples erected in the age of Pericles, but Greek beauty was cold and formal compared with the Gothic votive offerings.

Rome and Italy were always inclined toward the classical style of ancient Rome and Greece. It is not, then, surprising that a revival of classical building should finally have come in the fourteenth and fifteenth centuries — a period of truly great genius in architecture, sculpture, and painting.

The religious revolt of the sixteenth century disturbed the peace of Europe and put an end to the quiet beauty of devotion. The discovery of America brought an era of exploration and commerce. Religion declined, fervor of devotion cooled, and beauty was no longer an accompaniment of worship.

And here let me enunciate at once a great historic truth. Ages of great faith have always been in the Church ages of the love for beauty. On the contrary, where beauty was less sought or loved, it seems that religion also was at a low ebb.

A few years ago we boasted of the twentieth century as an age of science, material comfort, and progress. There is a possibility that people of the future may look back upon the beginning of this century as a great spiritual age also. The saintly Pope Pius X started a religious revolution when he prepared to "renew all things in Christ." He encouraged a new interest in the public prayer and ceremonies of the Church. The response was slow, for the indifference of four centuries could not be overcome in a single Pontificate. But a response was

not wanting. Here and there a new interest in public worship developed and finally there was born what was known
as the "Liturgical Movement." It is this which has been
leading back the people to a truer evaluation of the Mass, of
church music, processions, the frequentation of the sacraments,
and to a loving interest in the continual novelty of the Church's
calendar. By a natural process of reasoning there next developed
also a new interest in the external forms of religion. Interest in
ceremonies led to interest in the place where these were to be
performed. It was soon realized that a dark and slovenly furnished church was not the place for beautiful vestments and solemn liturgical acts. So ecclesiastical art was included in the movement for a more perfect expression of public worship. But by art
we do not here mean the mere reproduction of the creations of
other nations and other times, frozen forms, but the expression
of beautiful thought in sensible form, prompted by a new desire
for worthiness, not only in external appearance but of innate
quality.

For the first time people began to realize that their churches
failed to answer their high purpose. Once they began to give
heed to the externals of religion they realized that they had either
neglected their places of worship, or had lavished money and
effort on buildings that were vulgarly gaudy, showy, and pretentious. In the latter instance, builders of churches not satisfied with
merit unrecognized, were making nervous efforts, like the newly
rich, to attract attention. If the church structure is a declaration
of faith, then a dark, unshapely building, or a gaudily ornamented one, gives no hint of belief in the Real Presence.

As the Liturgical Movement rejected frivolous, theatrical effects
in music, so it naturally followed that men came to feel ashamed
also of shallow pretense in the designing of altars and the painting of walls. In the beginning of the century, a book on church
building and ornament would have gone without readers. Now,

thank God! there is general interest in the worthiness of the church to truly answer its high purpose.

In the past few years many beautiful and substantial churches have been erected. Priests and people find real enjoyment and inspiration in the sight of a well-designed church. The place of worship has come to be more perfectly, as it was in the distant past, a sacramental, to increase devotion. A few conservatives may continue to look upon art and architecture as an irrelevant fad, interfering with the spirit of real religion, but their conversion will not be long delayed. Only propriety is desired, and surely all sincere people wish that. Ugliness and vulgarity cannot represent fervent faith in the ancient Church. All sterling characters will wish a genuine representation of their religion in the edifices that proclaim it to the world.

There are, of course, artists who attempt to work in religious subjects without sharing in the spirit of worship, but they are not to be taken seriously. They are like writers who have tried to explain the beauty of great cathedrals of the past by proportion, variety, and the skill of trained artisans. If the purpose is missed, all is missed. An era of great church building is a time of great faith. Where the intention is unworthy, the fault will be recognized, even after many centuries, by every beholder. So, the appeal for better churches means a more earnest devotion which will be shown unconsciously in external forms. Sincere people, who have given to the world an appearance of insincerity, will remedy the fault when their attention is called to it. We are not interested in schools of art as much as in honesty of construction and unpretentious beauty of form. We do not urge the use of more costly material but of more logic and sincerity.

Argument from Sacred Scripture

We know from Sacred Scripture that there is a connection between beauty and worship. When the Israelites were crossing the

[4]

desert they could have no permanent temple, but the temporary tabernacle was surrounded with rich ornament. "Thou shalt make also a veil of violet and purple, and scarlet twice dyed, and fine twisted linen, wrought with fine embroidered work and goodly variety."[1]

And later, when they had established a permanent home in Judea and Solomon was building a temple of unprecedented splendor, the Scripture says of it: "And all the walls of the temple round about he carved with divers figures and carvings: and he made in them cherubims and palm trees, and divers representations, as it were, standing out, and coming forth from the wall. And the floor of the house he also overlaid with gold within and without."[2]

God has not changed. If in ancient times He was pleased by a temple of choice cedars and precious metals and carved ornament, He can still be honored in this way. The church is an offering to God to give Him the honor due from the creature to the Creator. It would fulfill its purpose if there were no worshipers within. But it has as a secondary purpose, the inspiration of devotion. A beautifully carved statue that may have been hidden away on the roof, is a sacrificial offering to God; but the statues and other ornaments on the interior are meant to be seen by man and to aid him in lifting his mind to God. That is the purpose of beauty in God's house. Its object is entirely spiritual. If strangers call it art, that is accidental. It is intended to please God and aid devotion.

In fact, it is thought by some writers that all art is religious in origin. Primitive men erected plain huts and made undecorated pottery. But to keep away evil spirits or to placate the Good Spirit they began to use ornamental designs representing spiritual

---

[1]Exodus xxvi. 31.
[2]III Kings vi. 29, 30.

[5]

things. One tribe taught another and one nation handed down its traditions to another nation, which in turn added to and improved them. Within historic times no art has been entirely original. It has always borrowed something from the past.

Primitive art was noted for its simplicity. It lacked perfection, but appealed by the humility of those who fashioned it. The Greeks developed art and architecture to earthly perfection, but it remained earthly only. They erected temples of flawless beauty, but merely to shelter statues of gods who were a purely human creation.

When at last, the new Christian civilization developed, there was a new inspiration given to art. The church became the center of Christian life, and within its walls was the tabernacle of God dwelling among men. Not even the temple of Solomon could claim the Sacramental Presence. Hence, in their full development, the Christian churches had reason to be more beautiful than the glorious temple of the Old Law itself. They were in all truth sacrificial offerings of the best marble and stone, the best carving and designing that mankind could bestow, for they were meant to give honor to God. They were built by the people of an age of great faith and noble deeds. From that time on the world has progressed in a material way only. Spiritually it has declined.

A spiritual revival, then, a restoration of all things in Christ, must almost of necessity include the love of beauty in the church. It is true that saints like Francis of Assisi have prayed fervently in an abandoned stable. Yet even that seraphic lover of Lady Poverty was in future years to inspire the beautiful frescoes of Giotto, which ornament the walls of the church where the saint himself now lies entombed. The Christians of the days of Roman persecution were willing to worship God in a private home, or in cemeteries, or in any place available, but although deprived of the possibility of erecting worthy churches, they decorated the walls of their places of worship with symbols of the sacraments and with disguised representations of the cross.

There have been ages of great art and little faith, but the churches in those periods fell short of perfection. The revival of paganism in the fifteenth century was a great artistic movement, but it lacked the religious spirit. It is easily possible to distinguish the difference. Paganism loved art for art's sake. Christianity used it for God's sake. When artists became proud of their work they ceased to be spiritual. Crude workmen, of an earlier day, who prayed before they worked, produced Church art which after many centuries can still bring the beholder to his knees in the Sacramental Presence.

Art is quite secondary to devotion, but in times of great spirituality it was an outward sign of inward faith. There may have been Christians in those days who walked past the works of famous masters unseeingly, but they were few. The completion of a new picture by a master was a reason for rejoicing by the whole town. It was the greatest event in the lives of those people.

Absolutely speaking, a spiritual revival could conceivably be brought about without arousing interest in the externals of religion, but human nature, constituted as it is, can be lifted up by beauty of sight and sound to beauty also of thought.

Sanctity and Dignity of the Temple

There is a close relation between improvement in church building and the reform of church music. To quote from the *Motu Proprio* of Pope Pius X on Church Music:

"Filled as we are with a most ardent desire to see the true Christian spirit flourish again in every respect and to be preserved by all the faithful, we deem it necessary to provide before aught else for the sanctity and dignity of the temple, in which the faithful assemble for no other object than that of acquiring this spirit from its foremost and indispensable source."

[7]

"The sanctity and dignity of the temple!" "The foremost and indispensable source" of "the true Christian spirit!" The temple of worship should be made worthy of its high purpose. Not only is church music to be dignified and devotional, but the building itself should be an appropriate background. In form, color, and ornament, it should be an inspiration to prayer and a fitting offering to God. If theatrical music is improper, so is theatrical ornament. In the words of the great reformer on the Chair of Peter, the faithful should be able to acquire "the true Christian spirit" from the church.

The church building is a sacramental. Its purpose, besides being a place of worship, is to aid devotion. This is the reason why, from Apostolic times to the present, churches have been ornamented. Both simple and pretentious churches had the walls covered with pictures. Medieval Gothic churches were devotional in their very structure. Their inspiration came from nature. Their high arches imitated the meeting branches of the forest, and their carved ornaments took leaves and flowers as motifs.

There was no careful calculation of the actual space needed. Even small towns erected great churches as votive offerings. The spirit of the people was lifted up with the ascending walls of stone, while souls were inspired to better living by the hallowed atmosphere of Christian devotion that abode within them. Even after the lapse of centuries, tourists are driven to their knees by that atmosphere of religion more than by the beauty itself of the sacred offerings of an age of great faith.

The spirit of reverence is not easily attained. It must be sincere to be convincing. Copying of ancient cathedrals will not bring to a modern age the spirit of faith. Somewhere architect and workmen will fail to understand, and therefore will fail to attain the medieval fervor. The very act of copying is an admission of unworthiness. An original effort would be more sincere. It might not have the high artistic merit of the great Gothic cathedrals,

[8]

but it would have the merit of being at least an honest offering of our best.

At the present time non-Catholic churches are being built in medieval Gothic style, despite its inappropriateness for them, since it belongs to a different tradition. At the same time Catholics are less interested in the Gothic style, much as they admire the superhuman genius of the Gothic builders in an age of knighthood and of chivalry. But they realize that the Gothic style, at least in its more ornate form, does not represent the present age and that worship is not limited to any certain form of church.

The beginning of the Gothic revival in England was a High Church movement in the Anglican Church. The Catholic Pugins were invited in to design churches which would recall the days when all England was Catholic. Only the Gothic style could do that. The Renaissance or a new style would inspire no such associate idea. Only a Gothic church could represent interest in the medieval Church in England. As the symbol of a movement there could be no other choice.

With Catholics there is more freedom. We are interested in the old but equally in the new. The contemporary Church is as important as the medieval.

Here in America there is little reason for the Gothic style as the symbol of a High Church movement, as such a tendency is not noticeably strong. And there is less reason for the construction of liturgical buildings for nonliturgical Churches. Catholic liturgy is a way of honoring Christ in His Eucharistic Presence. That is the explanation of the rich variety of Gothic carving and of the fine marble of the Renaissance. When a Catholic church is being repaired, the Blessed Sacrament is removed and Catholics then talk in the church and do not kneel when they enter. Non-Catholic churches do not reserve the Blessed Sacrament and are, therefore, non-liturgical. Thirteenth-century Gothic does not represent Protestant belief or worship and is, therefore, illogical.

Appropriate design for an Evangelical church would emphasize preaching, singing, and social work. This is done by grouping Sunday school and other meeting rooms around an auditorium. Their plan is more logical than the copy of a Catholic church without the altar.

The more common use of religious pictures in non-Catholic churches in recent years is a praiseworthy advance. It is the best way of representing to the eye the spirit of devotion.

"It is the spirit that quickeneth." The sacred, devotional atmosphere may pervade any style of church. It is tangibly expressed by the genuineness of material, the excellence of furnishings and the good taste displayed in them, all religiously prompted by reverence for the House of God. In the past, many parishes have been, one might almost say, maligned by architects and decorators, that is, truly religious people have been represented in the sight of God and man as lovers of sham and of pretense. The Liturgical Movement will lead to more care in the selection of artists who are to accomplish a work so closely connected with worship. The "dignity of the temple" has been the object of many rules issued by the Congregation of Rites. At one time altars were covered by electric bulbs of various colors, used in connection with the wax candles upon the altar, and forming odd designs. This was forbidden as being undignified and theatrical. Readers will recall other similar rules.

In recent buildings more attention is given to material, location, cost, and purpose than to the blind following of an ancient style. Churches have a liturgical purpose which should control the design. Thus some, for instance, are for intimate gatherings of a united group such as the nuns within a convent chapel. Intimacy can here be correctly represented by a low, flat ceiling, by the carpeted floor, and warm colors in the decoration. For a time, in the early Church, round and octagonal buildings were used, with the altar in the center. This was later abandoned for the

Basilican type, which is meant for larger assemblies. The transept of a cruciform basilica allowed worshipers to gather around the altar.

Height is necessary for dignity and formality. A cathedral without a high ceiling is unthinkable. A large sanctuary is likewise necessary for a cathedral. This is required not only to provide room for great functions, but to lend dignity to the edifice.

Processions, too, are now being given more recognition and the design of the church should consequently provide aisles sufficiently wide for this purpose.

A small parish cannot afford to build high vaults in the cathedral manner, and it should therefore not strive for the unattainable. A parish church with a low ceiling is more homelike and has the merit of suitability to conditions.

Wall decoration has a great deal to do with the devotional atmosphere of a church. Solemn and dignified ceremonies are impossible in a church with frivolous and distracting ornament. In an age which loves plainness and directness, a church decorated with the riotous flowering of the Baroque style would fail to impress the worshiper. In the same way, beautiful ceremonies could not redeem a church furnished in bad taste. The white walls of an unfinished church would be far better, for there would be here at least possibilities of improvement.

The purpose of church ornament, as defined above, is to honor God and to inspire devotion in the worshipers. There is a third purpose, however, which, though perhaps of less importance, should not be overlooked: the Church has a missionary mandate. She must bring to all mankind the glad tidings of salvation. How can this be done to the best effect if the outward appearance of her edifices is made repellant? The Church represents Christ, Who was attractive in His appeal to men. Our churches, then, should be worthy of what outwardly they represent before the world. The Church in America has never properly

represented its cause. Catholics have done their full share in building and defending the nation and in rendering public service,
but they have contributed little to the culture of the nation. Like
their neighbors, they have neglected the arts. But the Church is
by tradition the main patron of the arts. Hereafter, then, by the
improvement of our architecture, painting, and sculpture, we can
make a true contribution to the betterment of humanity and thus,
in turn, a missionary appeal for the cause of Christ.

But not only things within the church are suggestive of religion. The church building itself is a symbol. It represents the
Church of Christ on earth, so in a manner Christ Himself. Its
purpose is not merely to give shelter. It is more than merely a
sacramental to aid devotion. Christ left the Universal Church
on earth to take His place; to teach His doctrines, admin-
ister His sacraments, and apply to the souls of men His grace
gained by the Redemption. The Church continues His life; heal-
ing, consoling, and redeeming. The first man took the human
race away from God but Christ brought it back and left the
Church to preserve a bond of unity between earth and heaven.
Christ is invisible now to earthly eyes but His spiritual and invisible Church has a visible body. It has earthly leaders and
earthly subjects. And where its members gather they are united
in the public worship of God by the Universal Church in a building which represents the Church of Christ to that locality. For
this high purpose it must be a worthy representative. To fail in
that would be sacrilegious. The church building need not have
the riches of earth but it must have those of heaven. It must have
power, spirituality, beauty, and perpetuity.

The church is no common hall. It is to house members of a
spiritual organization which is the mystical body of Christ. It is
not merely a place of worship. It is the scene and setting for the
most sublime acts. Within it the Sacrifice of the Cross is renewed
in an unbloody manner in the Sacrifice of the Mass. At the bap-

tismal font the grace of God is to be applied to regenerated souls. From the altar is to flow a seven-branched stream of spiritual life and strength. The church is not merely a place of devotion. Men are here made to participate in the gifts of grace which Christ Himself has purchased for them by His Passion and Death.

When Christ assumed human nature He took a perfect human body without spiritual or physical blemish. His mystical Body is the faithful. The Church building is sacred to this worship and houses Christ Himself. It therefore should be as nearly perfect as possible. Evidently the designer and builders of a church should be men of prayer. They should approach their work with the reverence of acolytes lighting the candles for divine worship. They are participants in the priesthood. One who thinks of his task as of the designing of an auditorium is unsuited to the task. He is a guest who has come in without a wedding garment.

An austere, coldly furnished church is unsuited for music and ceremonies. Brick or stone interiors, without any contrast of ornament, are not conducive to devotion. They may be redeemed, however, by brilliant windows, carved furniture, and lively colors in pictures.

The latest designs of churches are well suited to the liturgy, since they delight in variety, as does the Church calendar. Plain mass is set off by bits of rich decoration to relieve the eye and elevate the soul. On the exterior, plain wall mass is relieved by window grouping and an ornamental portal. Interior walls are plain masses of color with a few bits of ornament for contrast, and the sanctuary is a grand climax of richness magnified by its juxtaposition with blank wall space. In the days of "all-over" patterns the effect was lost by tiring the eye. But with the more sparing use of ornament it is refreshed by the relief thus given, while at the same time we have an appropriate setting created for the sublime poetry and drama of the Mass.

The baptismal font should be discussed in the consideration of liturgical construction. Both the ceremony itself of baptism and the Church's tradition require the baptistry to be at the church entrance. At one time it was a separate building in front of the church but now it is merely outside the nave. It should not occupy an unused corner under the stairway leading to the choir, unless it can be given a proper dignity by carefully planned design and ornament. Prominence of location and beauty of decoration would show respect for that great sacrament which is the beginning of spiritual life.

To preserve the dignity of the sanctuary, there should be a way of going to the sacristy other than through the sanctuary. This is usually provided, but there are exceptions. The sanctuary should be entered only for ceremonies — a Holy of Holies.

As regards the location of the choir, there is room for discussion. When mixed choirs were used it became the custom to have a choir loft in the rear of the church. A liturgical choir might be given a place of greater prominence. It is not necessary that singers be seen, but the same reasoning which requires the baptismal font at the entrance would give the choir a place of prominence in the church, since the members take part in public worship. Where a male choir, and especially a vested choir, sings proper liturgical music, there would seem to be justification for placing it in the sanctuary. When the choir is placed in the sanctuary or in front of the church, it is required that it be a male vested choir. In ancient monastic chapels the monks occupied choir stalls in the sanctuary and not all of them were priests. Moreover, they had no part in the ceremonies except by singing.

Sometimes, in medieval churches, the choir was placed immediately in front of the sanctuary railing, outside the sanctuary, as, for example, in the Basilica of San Clemente in Rome, where the choir is surrounded by a marble wall of about the same height as the Communion rail. In this location the position of the organ would present a difficulty. For that reason, if the choir is to be located near the sanctuary, it seems well to give it a position at one side, in the place often used as the acolytes' sacristy. This will then be the best practical solution of the problem.

Dignity and reverence will be attained by beautiful vestments and worthy altar furnishings. It is a praiseworthy custom to have vestments made by ladies of the parish. They can thus be made different in design from purchased vestments and will, moreover, be a sacrificial offering, sharing in the spirit which animated the Catholic populations of those medieval towns, where the men worked at the construction and beautifying of their churches, while the women made the embroidered vestments, taking more pleasure in seeing articles of rich handiwork in the church than in the home.

There is room, too, for improvement in metal work, in the design and ornamentation of sacred vessels and altar furnishings. There has been too much glitter and showiness, too much piling up of flashy effects. As a remedy, the making of special designs has been proposed. That would be commendable, but small parishes cannot hire the best artists to draw up plans for every piece of furnishing needed. After all, the fault is not so much with standardization as with the repetition of poor designs. An improvement at the source would make better altar furnishings available to all churches. Nevertheless, wherever it can be afforded, a special design is a more perfect offering to worship as it is a more desirable contribution to art.

Hearing of the rich vessels of the church, thieves sometimes break in and steal chalices. But when melted down their spoils prove to be no more than a mass of worthless metal. In material and workmanship the Holy Grail should truly be worthy of its noble purpose.

The confessional should have a sacramental appearance inside as well as outside. It should be soundproof, heated, and ventilated. Usually the exterior is sufficiently ornate, but the interior is rough and unfinished. Within it a sacrament is received and the appearance should aid devotion. The deadening of sound may be easily effected by modern methods of construction and it will prevent irreverence.

Symbolism

In the very beginning of the Church the custom sprang up of representing doctrine by symbols. During the days of Roman persecution the "discipline of the secret" prevailed which required that the mysteries of the Faith should be hidden from unbelievers. On the walls of the catacombs were pictured symbols which could mean nothing to pagan spies or the uninitiated who might chance to see them, yet which were full of meaning to the faithful.

Strange as it may appear at first glance, some of these symbols had even a pagan connotation before a new meaning was attached to them by the Christians. Time is required for the development of a system of art, and so pagan vines and garlands were pictured and given a Christian significance. The swastika, an oriental symbol, was used to represent the cross.

When persecution ceased, the custom of employing symbols still continued. Comparisons were taken from the parables, the psalms, and the writings of the Fathers of the Church. Symbols were further gathered from sermons and hymns and utilized for the figurative illustration of Christian doctrines. Saints were represented by objects which might best recall the events of their life or martyrdom. Before the invention of printing, people, in fact, were largely taught by pictures. The walls of churches were covered by representations of events from the Bible and by doctrinal symbols which were studied and understood by the people.

Three of the best-known symbols were popularized by the Emperor Constantine. They are the cross and the two monograms of Christ. Before that time the cross was a secret symbol only, but with the restoration of liberty to the Church and the abolition of crucifixion as a death penalty, the cross began to be used as a symbol surmounting the churches and on all articles connected with Christian worship. The crucifix had never been represented except symbolically, as for example, in the picture of a dolphin pierced by a trident. Now, however, it became a symbol of the resurrection and of the triumph over death on the part of Christ and of the triumph of His Church. In all later temples the cross is found over altars, over Stations of the Cross, and in the form of flowered finials at the top of Gothic spires. Even the four-leaved clover is a conventional symbol of the cross.

Constantine also rendered popular two monograms of Christ — one called the *Chi-rho,* which consists of the first two letters that occur in the Greek spelling of the name Christ — XP. The equivalent of these in our language would be the form, CHR. Often a cross was added to the symbol.

The other monogram dating from early days is the well-known symbol, IHS. This is similarly made up of the first three letters of the name, Jesus, as written in the Greek language, which we must remember, was the language of the early Church. As the knowledge of Greek, however, became less widespread, the letters were incorrectly made and have often been incorrectly interpreted. In our language the letters would be written, JES.

In medieval times this Holy-Name monogram was given great currency by St. Bernardine of Siena, who carried about with him a shield bearing this symbol. During his preaching he was wont to set it in a position of prominence, and it came in time to be placed over the doors of homes where the saint had preached.

The church building has a definite meaning. It represents Christ and His Church and should have a dignity and perfection worthy of that purpose.

The sanctuary, as the place of sacrifice, should be more ornate than other parts of the sacred edifice. The body of the church is called the "nave," from *navis,* boat, since the Church represents

[17]

the bark of Peter, which will carry its passengers safely through temporal storms to eternal happiness. The arch which separates the nave from the sanctuary is called the "arch of triumph." It symbolizes the passage from earth to heaven. In ancient churches a crucifix was suspended from the arch, or stood upon a rood loft, to represent the purchase of salvation by Christ's death on the cross, opening up to the faithful the heavenly sanctuary. Even the floor plan of the church was usually in the shape of a cross.

Although the material of which the church was constructed was not spiritual by nature, yet it could be given a spiritual meaning. When used for a church it was blessed and became a sacramental. This was true of everything in the church — walls, windows, doors, statues, pictures, colors, numbers, figures of flowers, birds, and animals, all were used to declare the glory of God.

This language of symbolism is almost unknown in America and should be better studied. Full recognition was given to it in the new Sacred Heart Church of Pittsburgh. It should be an important feature of every church. A complete discussion of symbolism and of the traditional way of representing virtues, vices, doctrines, etc., would be well worth while here, but the work has already been thoroughly done in a small volume called, *Church Symbolism* (Herder), written by M. C. Nieuwbarn, O.P., and translated by John Waterreus. Another book, *The World's Symbolism* (Hyland, 1916), by Ambauen, contains a long list of symbolic comparisons, mostly from literature but applicable also to art.

A tourist in Europe, spending an hour or two with an intelligent guide in one of the famous medieval churches, may learn a great deal about the Bible, Church history, and liturgy. Similarly, in a new parish church, the use of symbolism will elevate the soul above brick and mortar, will disengage it from earthly distractions, and aid it in devotion, while opening up a rich field for imagination and Christian piety.

[18]

Chapter II

THE BASILICA

THE first Christian church was a borrowed building. For the first celebration of the Eucharistic Rite the Apostles did not engage an architect. Instead they met a stranger who led them to the Upper Room.

In the earliest years of Christianity the building of churches was hardly possible. Hence, we have no Apostolic churches except a cave where St. Peter preached and baptized, a room where he said Mass, a dungeon made into a sanctuary by the presence of the saintly prisoners Peter and Paul, a residence of Aquila and Priscilla converted into a church, and later the churches built on sites that were still redolent with the memory of the Apostles.

During the three hundred years of persecution suffered by the Church there could be no permanent temples. A few were constructed in time of peace and destroyed in time of persecution, but from their ruins we can learn little except that a certain type of church building had been developed before peace came to the Church. The style thus introduced can here be briefly described.

There was, to begin with, a round apse for the altar. The nave was divided from the sanctuary and another division occurred toward the rear, behind which knelt the penitents and the unbaptized.

For safety, the early Christians usually were obliged to worship in the homes of the more well-to-do converts not suspected of being Christians. It was the custom for slaves and clients of wealthy Romans to call on them each morning to receive their orders for the day. In a similar manner, a group of Christians might readily enter a patrician residence on Sunday morning,

[19]

BASILICA OF SAN LORENZO, ROME

Fourth century. The narthex, or entrance porch, and the clerestory to heighten the nave are shown. Small windows. Plain exterior with pictures on front. The medieval tower was erected later.

without attracting attention. Underground cemeteries, too, were sometimes used as places of worship, but they were not excavated for that purpose and had but little room for any great number of worshipers. Private homes had neither ecclesiastical form nor decoration. They had plenty of space and secrecy, but that was all they could offer.

The catacombs themselves had no architectural form, but possessed crude decorations of Biblical scenes and symbolical representations of the sacraments and of Christian doctrine. Their chapels could hold no more than perhaps some twenty people, while the passages which led to them were narrow. Hence, they were used as places of worship for an anniversary Mass only, or in time of severe persecution when no gathering would be safe within the city walls.

Church building, therefore, dates from the time of the great Emperor Constantine who, as a prospective member of the Faith, finally led the Church out of her hiding, offered the Pope his imperial palace, and built above the tomb of St. Peter a large and beautiful Christian church.

The First Basilica

The first basilica was the result of a combination of circumstances. When Constantine became Emperor of Rome he invited Pope Miltiades to dwell with him in the Lateran palace until he could erect a new imperial structure for himself and leave the Lateran entirely to the Pope. Since there was need here of a chapel, the law court, or "basilica," as it was termed, of the palace was converted into a chapel and called the "Basilica of the Holy Savior." It is still the cathedral church of Rome and of the world, under the title of St. John Lateran.

The Lateran Basilica had five naves, and to each of these a door led from without. There were four rows of green marble pillars, while beautiful silver lamps lighted each nave. The walls were

INTERIOR, BASILICA OF SAN LORENZO, ROME

Pillars support the clerestory. Altar in the style commonly used previous to the tenth century. Early use of the baldachino which is proper in a modern church of any style except Gothic. Two pulpits or ambones. Mosaic floor.

pictured in frescoes, now no longer preserved, although a portion of the mosaic decorating the apse dates to the time of Constantine.

Wealth confiscated from the Church by former emperors was returned to her by Constantine for the purpose of erecting fitting houses of worship. The altar of the Lateran Basilica was thus enriched with precious stones and carving in marble and alabaster, while over it hung a canopy of solid silver, forcibly reminding us that the use of a canopy over the altar goes back even to that early date.

Churches were erected by Constantine in Rome, Byzantium, Bethlehem, Jerusalem, and Antioch. In this manner, too, he established a style of building which lasted for centuries in the West. In fact, it was used in Rome itself up to the time of the Renaissance. Rome taught the world not only the religion of Christ but the type of building in which He was to be worshiped. But a great deal of the credit for it all is deservedly Constantine's. His basilicas are still the most important of the sights of Rome.

Constantine had been in both the East and West. He had seen the Christian churches of the Orient which had escaped destruction, and those of Rome, which was now in its decline. For a century barbarian emperors had her destroyed rather than built up. Few artists were available. Yet somehow these few were found and set to work. So Rome made a new contribution to world architecture.

Greek temples were low of ceiling and incapable of development. Roman temples had been small, with room only for a statue and an incense tripod. The basilica was a new type of religious structure, beautiful in itself and capable of development. After many centuries it expanded into the glory of the Gothic cathedrals.

The basilica took its form partly from the public law courts and partly from the arrangements of private Roman homes used for worship in time of persecution. The name had been

[23]

sometimes used for Christian churches before the time of Constantine, possibly because the basilicas of the Forum were places of public assembly.

The Roman neophytes used a new form of structure for two reasons. In the first place, it was necessary to avoid everything pagan and therefore the style of pagan temples of worship could not be used. Secondly, these edifices were small, while the Christian churches must be large enough to hold great masses of people. The pagans were satisfied to have an official perform the rites of worship without the presence of the people whom he represented. Christians recognized an individual obligation. So, the patrician home expanded into a public building; it was called a basilica ("hall of the king"), and became the throne room of the heavenly King.

Had artists of that time been copyists they might have simply reproduced the form of Greek temples or else used the ancient basilicas as they found them. But even in an age of decadent art and architecture they chose to be original. They put a transept in the building and made it cruciform. They employed old basic ideas of structure in a new way and developed something not identified with paganism. The Lateran Basilica, St. Mary Major, St. Laurence, St. Clement, and the old Basilica of St. Peter were to have an influence on all future church building. Thus the name "basilica" implies not only a title of honor but also a style of architecture.

Features of the Basilica

The hall of the pagan basilica became the nave of the Christian church. The seat of the judge became the bishop's throne, and an altar was erected beneath the half dome of the apse. Penitents were obliged to collect alms at the church entrance, and so a porch, or *narthex,* was placed in front. It was usually low, with a lean-to roof. Separate from the building was a round or square bell tower. The earliest basilicas had a round baptistry outside, containing the tomb of some saint. Later a baptismal chapel was erected within the church and the tomb of the saint was placed beneath the main altar.

The secular basilica, as completed by Constantine and bearing his name, had round vaults in the ceiling. The Christians, however, chose to use instead a flat roof, but raised the ceiling of the central nave into a clerestory which gave variety to the outward design and light to the interior. It was a step forward from the unbroken flat ceiling of the original structure. The clerestory was now supported by columns. Its ceiling was still flat, but the height of the nave gave majesty to the interior. That idea of a high central nave and lower side aisle was retained in later styles. It has been little used in America but it is one of the most attractive features of ancient churches.

The ambulatory outside the two rows of pillars was not intended as seating space. It gave depth, shadow, and proportion to the building. The low roof at the sides made the roof of the central nave seem higher in contrast.

The roof trusses were usually covered by a wooden ceiling which was gilded or painted in polychrome. In some of the old basilicas the trusses are now visible but it is believed they were once covered by a wooden ceiling which was removed when it showed signs of decay.

The basilica was usually about twice as long as it was wide. The side aisles had about half the width and height of the nave. The church of St. Cecilia in Rome, which is a patrician residence turned into a church, has an atrium in front, surrounded by columns.

The best example of the ancient basilica is that of St. Apollinare in Classe, six miles south of Ravenna, at the place of the former port. The sea receded, the port was abandoned, and the basilica has not been used for many years. It is unchanged by restorations.

INTERIOR, BASILICA OF ST. PAUL OUTSIDE THE WALLS, ROME

Rebuilt in recent times. Old basilican arrangement, but Renaissance enrichment. Clerestory in nave. Lower side aisles beyond pillars. One baldachin with posts starting at corners of altar and a larger canopy above, in proportion

It has unity of style because its marble pillars were made for that church and not taken from some other building, as in the case of the Roman basilicas. The sanctuary of St. Apollinare is raised quite high above the floor of the nave and is approached by a series of about twelve steps. The altar is covered with a canopy supported by four pillars. The walls were decorated in mosaics in rich colors. The two rows of pillars support round arches. The wooden rafters of the roof are visible. Probably they were never inclosed, as the tie beams are irregular in surface and a flat wooden ceiling could not have been fastened to them.

The altars of the original basilicas were usually a block of marble, plainly ornamented, or a marble table. The apse, or sanctuary, was richly decorated in mosaic or fresco, since it was the place of honor which contained the altar, the bishop's throne, and the ciborium with the Blessed Sacrament. The arch which divided the nave from the sanctuary was next in richness of decoration, as it was the gateway to the sanctuary. A band of ornament stretched around the clerestory just below the windows. The windows which are now in the basilicas must have been a later innovation, for windows as we know them now were unknown in Apostolic times. Small pieces of glass or mica were used, while the perforations made to inclose them were highly ornamental.

St. Apollinare has a round bell tower separate from the church. Later, square towers were attached to the church. The bell towers or *campanili,* were the chief ornament of the medieval basilicas and at the present time thirty or forty of them are the main feature of the Roman skyline.

The floors of the basilicas were made quite ornamental, since there were no fixed seats. Panels of colored marble and stone formed the decorations, set off by spirals and other designs of small cubes in various colors. Circles of colored marble were obtained by sawing sections from old marble pillars. The walls were of stone or concrete, more often the latter. The concrete of that time was not reinforced and could not span wide spaces as now. Concrete walls required ornamentation and hence were incrusted in marble selected for its color and veining, or were covered with mosaic patterns composed of small cubes of marble, glass, and terra cotta. This sort of decoration is almost imperishable. Its colors are as fresh today as when they first were laid upon the wall. The mosaic pavement was an idea dating from pagan Rome. Mosaic wall decoration was also known by the Romans, but the decoration of churches in that way had its inspiration in the East. To be logical, the basilicas should have been decorated in the colors and symbolism of the catacombs. Perhaps they were; if so, this ornamentation did not last.

In the sixth century Rome had fallen into decay and Ravenna was now more important. Mosaic workers came from Constantinople and decorated the churches of both Rome and Ravenna in the style popular in the East. The figures of the saints were purposely made crude and unlifelike in order to satisfy the Iconoclasts, but the colors used were beautiful. Upon a gold and blue background was placed every imaginable color, and this without any vulgar display. The general effect inspired devotion.

We should not leave the discussion of early churches without a mention of other forms of design. Circular and octagonal plans were tried out, but never became very popular. Baptisteries built outside of churches were circular in form and this may have suggested that shape for churches. The altar was erected in the center. The same grouping of the people around the altar was, however, made possible by the use of a transept in a basilica. The altar was then placed at the crossing and the people could attend Mass on three sides of the altar.

Modern Basilicas

The purpose of this book is not historical but practical. It is our intention to omit whatever knowledge cannot be made useful at the present time. In choosing the style of architecture for a contemplated church building, we should consider the possibilities of the basilica style, since it is the first in the historical order.

Every Catholic should be interested in the traditions of his Church, and it should aid his devotion to realize on entering an American church built in this style, that he views the very design which was first thought out by Constantine the Great, under whom were brought to a termination the three long centuries of early persecution and martyrdom and who made Christianity the favored religion of the Roman Empire. Such a glorious association of ideas cannot be evoked to the same degree by any other style of church since all other forms were developed outside of Rome. The Renaissance, it is true, was also a Roman style, but for its inspiration it went back to pagan Rome. The basilica, on the contrary, is essentially Christian. It was the invention of the infant Church.

The basilican design was used to good advantage here in America by the late John Comes, who died while still in the midst of his splendid efforts to free Catholic art from the shackles of inferiority. He pointed out the promised land, but left the leadership to others. Comes used several styles, but we are here interested in the basilica alone. In a brochure, published by him and entitled *Catholic Art and Architecture,* we find pictures of St. Mary's, at McKeesport, Pa., of St. Monica, at Rochester, N. Y., and an exterior view of St. Mary's, at St. Cloud, Minn., which were all built in the Basilican style. At St. Cloud, the *narthex,* or entrance porch, is used, but it is omitted at Rochester.

In the interiors of these churches the ambulatories are narrowed to aisles and all the pews are contained between the pillars. Thus the pillars add to the beauty of the church, but do not obstruct the view.

It is difficult to improve on the plan of two rows of pillars which form a vista leading to the sanctuary and main altar. The

ST. MARY'S CHURCH, ST. CLOUD, MINNESOTA

Nairne W. Fisher, Architect, St. Cloud, Minn.

Shows modern use of the basilican plan; has entrance porch, high nave, and lower side aisles.

eye is carried directly to the center of interest. The plan is used everywhere except in America, but Americans must have an auditorium with unobstructed view. They might get away from that idea if they learned to think of the church as a house of prayer rather than a place to attend Mass, hear a sermon, and then hurry home. Pillars give depth and shadow to the church, and a quiet spot in the shadow of a lofty pillar is a better place for prayer and meditation than an open auditorium.

We admit, however, that pillars, while at one time structurally necessary, are not so now. The ancient builders could not possibly span a wide space, so pillars were required to support the roof. Modern engineering skill can bridge any space and so they are no longer necessary from that point of view. But even now it remains easier and cheaper to build a roof supported by pillars, so that this would still be the less costly method of construction, unless the distance of shipping the marble should render the expense too great. The Basilican style could not, however, be used without pillars or piers, inasmuch as the clerestory must have some visible means of structural support.

The windows in a modern basilica should be somewhat small and conventional in design. Pictured windows are Gothic in origin and Gothic windows cannot be used in a somewhat classical church. The windows should be designed for the church and should not be merely stock windows cut down to fill the space desired.

Modern churches in the Basilican style are usually decorated in the Byzantine, or Oriental, style of the original basilicas. This style of decoration was foreign in Rome and is doubly so here. We have little connection with sixth-century Constantinople, although we may logically adopt anything from ancient Europe. We may use the formal simplicity of the ancient basilicas, but the figures should then be contemporary in design. We cannot expect people who have not seen the original basilicas to be interested in a style of decoration which probably seemed strange at first even to the Romans.

The Benedictine monks of Beuron Abbey, in Germany, have developed a style of mural decoration very appropriate for a basilica. They use the colors and the solemn dignified forms of ancient classical art, with some of the grandeur of the ancient Egyptians, but the faces are modern, so that we behold here not a dead but a living style. It will be treated at greater length in Chapter X on Interior Decoration.

Mosaic decoration cannot be imitated in paint. The two are distinctly different mediums. Painting squares in gold or colors to imitate mosaic is dishonesty. The colors of the past may be used, but why should painted decoration pretend to be something which it is not? If we cannot afford mosaic walls, we should be satisfied with painted ones, without imitation. Even a hint of archaic design may be justified, but crudeness is repellant. We can overlook faults in ancient decoration, but for moderns to be intentionally crude is unpardonable.

Mosaic decoration is the most beautiful and lasting of any form of applied ornament. It is illogical construction, but beautiful decoration. The rough surface makes it seem unpretentious. Nature never makes a mistake in color, and the natural colors of marble and stone are always sufficiently subdued. The finer figure work can be done by artists only, but the background could be done by common workmen under the supervision of a designer. The ancient Romans were like Americans in desiring buildings to be constructed as much as possible by common labor. They taught the provincials of Gaul and Britain to build as well as the Romans themselves. We have few mosaic workers now in America, but if there were a demand there would be a supply of workers. To copy a stilted, unreal style is not living art. Mosaics, however, can be used in any style of mural decoration in any style of church — Gothic, Renaissance, or modern.

THE BASILICA

A stone wall, unadorned except by carving, would be, it is true, a more logical construction. Mosaic is an incrustation on a concrete wall and, to a certain extent, misrepresents, although there is no intention to deceive. Instead of covering an entire wall, mosaic could be used in small spaces for contrast and the unornamented space would show the wall with its own homely virtues, undisguised and unpretending.

CATHEDRAL OF ST. MARK, VENICE

Eleventh and twelfth centuries. The roof is broken up into domes, some of which are shown here.
Rich ornament of the East.

Chapter III

BYZANTINE CHURCHES

WHEN Constantine moved the capital of the empire from Rome to Byzantium, Rome began to decline and Byzantium became the center of imperial splendor. Architects from Rome and from all the provinces were brought in to the new capital to erect churches and palaces. There, then, the Roman style of building first adopted some of the forms and colors of the East.

The city of Rome remained loyal to the basilica, and some basilicas were erected also in the eastern capital. In general, however, an eastern type of building prevailed in the new capital, from which it received its name "Byzantine," although Byzantium itself had previously been a small city, without any traditions of art or architecture. The style continued supreme during the following seven centuries.

The term "Byzantine style" now simply means the Oriental style. Owing to political and commercial influences it spread through the West wherever Constantinople had developed its interests. Oriental churches were erected in Ravenna, Venice, and Genoa. In Rome the structural forms were not used in external designs, but the interiors of the older basilicas were decorated with mosaic in the rich, dark colors of the East.

The Byzantine style departed from the long nave of the Basilican type and used various shapes. It might be circular, octagonal, square, or in the form of a Greek cross. Whatever the shape, the center was crowned by a dome, which admitted light into the interior, gave it height and dignity, and provided a central axis. Classical Roman architecture had used vaults and domes, and the Roman basilicas still remained typically Roman, and yet with the evidences of a new development. The Byzantine movement was almost entirely Oriental.

A recent writer, Joseph Strzygowski, has attempted to trace the origin of Christian art in Persia and in the countries under its influence. (*Origin of Christian Church Art,* Clarendon Press, Oxford.) While it is true that an enemy empire could not expect to exert a great influence, yet some effects at least were thus produced by Syrian art. The earlier Christian persecutions did not seriously affect Syria and so churches continued to be erected there, while Roman Christians were obliged to worship secretly.

Constantine spent his early life in Nicomedia and when he assumed imperial power over Rome he was somewhat familiar with the Christian churches of the East. He had at least seen the exteriors and was able to help in the design of the Roman basilicas. Later, the influence of Constantinople helped to preserve the wide popularity of richly colored mosaics, but such decoration, we must remember, had already been used by the Classical Romans. The formalism of Byzantine ornamentation thus prevailed for many centuries in the Western Church, but structurally the style had nothing to offer. When the new Christian civilization began to emerge and to develop church architecture, it ignored the Byzantine style and went back to the Roman Basilican.

The great example of the Byzantine style is the former church, now a mosque, of *Hagia Sophia* (Divine Wisdom), built by Justinian in Constantinople. All lines here converge into an immense dome, perfect in symmetry and occupying the place of the entire ceiling. In plan and ornamentation it is one of the great architectural beauties of the world. Designers of other churches, however, divided the ceiling into several domes. This is but another variation of the Roman round-arch vaulting. Not being able to build entirely of marble, they lined the interior with a thin marble veneer and with mosaic decoration in bits of variously colored stone brought together from all the provinces. Thus, a structure of dull brick and concrete became a lasting glory of saints and angels and religious symbols, worked out in colored marble on a background of blue and gold.

St. Mark's of Venice

The best example of the Byzantine style in western Europe is St. Mark's of Venice, which might also be considered as belonging to the Orient. St. Mark's is not merely the greatest sight in Venice; it *is* Venice. Both commerce and pleasure are centered around the Cathedral square, and carried on under the shadow of the Lion of the Evangelist. Around the square are pillared arcades serving as an approach to the heavenly vision. At the end of the square rises a domed pyramid, opalescent in the sunlight. Here one stands, lost in wonder, as he looks on the elusive colors of the East, "poured into her lap" eight centuries ago, when Venice "sat in state."

As one enters from the brilliant outdoors, he suddenly finds himself for a moment in a darkness pierced only by a few rays of light from small windows in the domes and from burning lamps about the altar. Slowly, then, the interior becomes visible, like the development of an Alpine sunrise.

The interior is cross shaped. It is divided by massive piers into mysterious recesses. Every inch of wall space is covered by an incrustation of jasper, porphyry, alabaster, and serpentine in a wonderful blending of color, taught by artists from Constantinople but readily learned by the Venetians, who became masters of color combination.

One might spend hours in enjoyment of the very atmosphere as the rays of afternoon light pass from one picture group to another, revealing saints and symbols. Some figures are stilted, but that only adds to their solemnity. One might ignore the pictures and enjoy the combinations of blue and green, purple and red, blended with artistic instinct. But to behold it at its very best,

[37]

INTERIOR, CATHEDRAL OF ST. MARK, VENICE

Heavy piers uphold the domes. Altar with the first reredos. The color harmonies of mosaic walls cannot be shown in black and white.

one must view it in the quiet hours of early morning, in the company of devout worshipers, when it bursts on the entranced eyes like a glimpse of the beatific vision.

Modern Adaptation

It is all most beautiful, and yet it is not meant for us to copy. The subtle, sacred aura of a thousand years cannot be imitated. The style cannot be adopted as the plan of modern parish churches. It is indeed Catholic, but of another age and another race. We may use it in rare instances, but it is not a universal style. We learn from it, however, the importance of color. Cold, gray walls are not an aid to the prayerful spirit, but, when irreverent tourists are not at hand to distract the impulse of devotion, there is a power in these rich, yet subdued colors of St. Mark's to force one to his knees.

Taught at length the secret of logical construction by the Gothic cathedral builders, we cannot now go back to the dead weight of a cluster of domes, supported by heavy piers and Cyclopean walls. The dome is better than a flat ceiling, but support by arches in the Romanesque manner is a superior method. After the development of Romanesque vaulting and Gothic spires, it would be a backward step to return to Byzantine domes, thick walls, marble incrustation, and low, dark interiors. The Byzantine revival produces higher, brighter interiors, but if we like that style on account of mosaic decoration, we may use mosaics in a church of Romanesque or any other style, excepting Gothic alone, which must be of logical construction. There is no historical or structural reason and scarcely any esthetic reason for the use of the Byzantine style at present. Strictly speaking, the modern churches said to be in the Byzantine style are really in the Romanesque style with Byzantine ornament.

One of the first modern churches erected in the Byzantine style is the cathedral of Marseilles, France, which was begun in 1852.

ST. LOUIS CATHEDRAL, ST. LOUIS, MISSOURI

Barnett, Hayes, and Barnett, Architects, St. Louis, Mo.

The dome which is the center of interest, has greater height than in the original Byzantine style. Detail is Romanesque. Granite has dignified contrast with green tile of the dome.

The exterior walls have alternate rows of green and white stone
— an Oriental idea in ornament. The two bell towers are topped
by domes and there are five other domes; the central dome over
the crossing, one over each transept, one over the choir, and one
over the chapel of the Blessed Virgin. The ceiling is higher than
in the ancient models of that style and the interior is much
brighter. The general appearance is not Oriental and the cathedral may be considered Romanesque as much as Byzantine.

This style was chosen for the new Westminster cathedral, in
London, by the late John Francis Bentley, one of the leaders in
the improvement of church architecture. He designed many
beautiful and original churches throughout England, but after
designing the London cathedral did not live to see its dedication. The exterior is a pyramid of alternate layers of stone and
dark-colored brick, dominated by a beautiful tower, 284 feet in
height. The tower is Byzantine in ornament, but its height is a
modernization. The main portal is in the form of a round arch.
The central dome is not seen from the front view but there are
many small domes on turrets. There is a set-back effect, remarkably coördinated, keeping the tower as the climax of interest.
The one criticism sometimes made has reference to darkness of
material both inside and out. A brighter color would certainly
have been more inspiring.

Concrete was used for domes, vaulting, and piers. At the time,
this was really an innovation in church building, since the cathedral had been begun just before the end of the past century, when
concrete construction was uncommon in any building and above
all for churches.

Within, the church is cruciform, but the length and height of
the nave are emphasized as in the Gothic churches. This is a decided improvement over the ancient Byzantine with its crushing
ceilings. Following the Byzantine traditions, the interior walls of
the cathedral are plated with variously colored marble and with

mosaics. The baldachino over the main altar attracts the eye by its Oriental splendor of alabaster and rare marble, of pearl and gold. Altogether, the structure is a great achievement in modern church architecture. It has transformed an ancient style into a modern style, for the church is not of the past but decidedly of the present.

St. Louis Cathedral

Probably a greater artistic triumph is the cathedral of St. Louis, Missouri, designed by the late George D. Barnett. Its dome of gray granite and green tile is a vision of beauty from afar. In place of the low flat domes of ancient times, this dome rises higher and lifts itself more lightly above the earth. The façade is flanked by two Romanesque towers, as the exterior is more Romanesque than Oriental. The ancient Byzantine style was a mixture of Eastern and Western ideas, and this new cathedral carries the development of the style up to the present time.

The interior is a paradise of harmonious color, of mosaic and marble, reaching its climax in the main altar under the beautiful and majestic baldachino. The jeweled windows, of American manufacture, immediately attract the eye. The predominating blue of one and red of the other are contrasted by the precious colors of the Orient. Art-glass windows were invented by Gothic builders and were not a feature of original Byzantine churches, but the St. Louis windows are correct in style and a pleasing addition to the Byzantine ornament.

The walls are rich in pictured mosaic of antique color combinations, but the figures are modern, that is, they have in them more of the modern than of the historic Byzantine formalism. With its inner walls thus entirely covered by imperishable mosaic, the St. Louis Cathedral holds high rank among the great cathedrals of the world.

INTERIOR, ST. LOUIS CATHEDRAL, ST. LOUIS, MISSOURI

Barnett, Hayes, and Barnett, Architects, St. Louis, Mo.

Sanctuary. The large baldachino is most proper in a Renaissance church, but was used in Italy in all churches including Byzantine and Romanesque. It is a form of canopy used to add dignity to the altar and make it the object of interest. That purpose is attained here.

[43]

ST. ANSELM'S CHURCH, NEW YORK, N. Y.

Gustave E. Steinback, Architect, New York, N. Y.

Brick construction with terra-cotta trim. Round arches stepped to a climax in a low dome.

INTERIOR, ST. ANSELM'S CHURCH, NEW YORK, N. Y.

Gustave E. Steinback, Architect, New York, N. Y.

Wide span with the dome only slightly interrupting the line of the arch. The interior is faced with tile instead of mosaics. The Benedictine medal is done in terra cotta, in colors. The decoration is in the Beuronese Style.

Not for Common Use

If, then, the most splendid cathedrals of the present generation have been erected in the Byzantine style, should that become the favorite style for all churches? By no means. It must of necessity be a cathedral style. It must be splendid or it fails. Walls must be plated with marble, which is not found locally and is expensive. Mosaic work is a trade not commonly practised by American workers. Imported labor might be a difficult problem. Americans could learn the art but it is too exotic. There is a preference now for keeping walls as they are and not giving them a false coating. We might build a dome-sheltered church and cover its interior walls with fresco, or painting, in the Byzantine style, but the design would be in discord with present taste. Our decorators, it is true, sometimes do attempt to paint in the Byzantine style, but without success. Painting cannot imitate mosaic, marble, or any other ornament. It must keep within its own limits.

Structurally the style has nothing to offer. It was outside the line of development which led from the Basilican to the Gothic style. There are better ways of treating ceilings than breaking them into domes which require massive support. Barrel vaulting, round and pointed arches are all better structural forms. But aside from the question of structure, the Byzantine style introduced into the Church the use of color, not promiscuous patches of color, but harmony of combinations and a general effect of beauty. Later builders often neglected to plan for the general effect, but the Orientals never lost sight of it. The style made a great contribution to church architecture, but it is too cumbersome, too expensive, too foreign, and too grand for common parochial use. It is a monumental style.

Chapter IV

THE ROMANESQUE STYLE

PROBABLY the church builders of past ages did not think of building according to any certain style. They used the best construction they knew for local materials and local workmen. When traveling was more difficult, each community built in its own way. The few who traveled to distant places brought back stories of something new in construction — a new use of pillars or curve of arch which had been tried in some church with good effect. It was introduced into the new community, but with variations according to local taste and building conditions. It was not a style; it was merely the best and most beautiful mode of construction known to the builders. Centuries later, art students found certain tendencies in certain places of the same date and they grouped these similar designs into what they called a style. It concerns historians rather than architects. Actual builders, if they have the artistic instinct, are not limited by what someone else did, but erect what seems to them logical, strong, and beautiful. By doing so, they make a contribution to the art of the ages.

During the formative period, when Europe was becoming civilized, new ideas of church building developed. There is considerable variety of design, but, for convenience, we group all the structural ideas from the decline of Rome until the development of the Gothic style in the twelfth and thirteenth centuries into what is called the Romanesque style. It did not originate in Rome. The name may have been given because the style developed in the former provinces of the Roman Empire.

After Constantine lost hope in Rome and started a new Eastern capital, Oriental influence predominated even in church building in Western Europe. Its records are seen mostly in the richly

FAÇADE, SÃO PAOLO, PISA, ITALY

Built in the Ninth Century; façade of the Twelfth Century. Called the old cathedral of Pisa. In the Lombard-Pisan style. The rose window was a Lombard invention, the arcades Pisan.

[48]

colored mosaics discussed in previous chapters. Roofs were broken up into domes, but it is uncertain whether the idea developed in the East or West, as domes were used in churches not of the Byzantine style.

The domes gave the idea of getting away from flat ceilings. The basilicas of an earlier age had flat ceilings of wood but they were subject to decay and fire, and during barbarian raids there was need of fireproof construction. But a flat ceiling could not be built of concrete or stone. Each stone required support from beneath. There was need of some sort of arch, and the domical ceiling solved that problem. The Byzantine domes were never generally used throughout the West. The barrel vault was tried, but where there was a transept the crossing of transept and nave made an awkward arrangement with barrel vaulting. Further, the spreading and falling in of roofs made it necessary to evolve a system of balance and proportion. Finally, ribbed vaulting came into use. Spreading was prevented by heavy piers in the side walls; sometimes by the walls of side chapels. Then buttresses were used, and at last flying buttresses. This logical system of support and balance and counter-thrust was the secret of Gothic style in a later century. The Gothic builders perfected the discovery of the Romanesque builders. Romanesque is sometimes called "Round-arch Gothic." The Gothic style is more graceful. The Romanesque is massive, crude, and undeveloped, but impressive with its strength, variety, and logical construction.

Originally Gothic was a term of contempt, meaning barbarian. It would have been more appropriate to call the Romanesque style barbarian, as it developed in unsettled times and had the rough crudeness of the woods. Gothic art was the perfected product of a new Christian civilization. Romanesque churches had for ornament only a little stone carving. There was scarcely any painted decoration, for the stone interior had no place for paintings. The crude carvings were poor art, but wonderful ar-

CHURCH OF NOTRE DAME, POITIERS, FRANCE

Built in the Twelfth Century. The carved ornament was originally in poly-chrome. Not as refined in detail as later churches, but rich in ornament and interesting in style, it has the crude beauty of the Romanesque. Pointed turrets and vertical lines are very near the Gothic style, but previous to its introduction.

chitecture, since the general effect was massive and majestic. Slender marble pillars were no longer used, but thick piers were substituted to sustain greater weight. The rib-vaulted ceiling was a great improvement in beauty and permanence over the flat ceiling of the basilica.

In place of the Basilican plan, with its high central nave and lower side aisles, a few churches in France used one nave only, with a series of chapels along each side which gave contrast to the design and an appearance of greater height to the nave. This construction drew attention away from the thick piers of the walls and effected a greater lightness of appearance. The same idea could be employed by us at present. We use a transept to break the long straight walls, but more variety is sometimes needed. A series of side chapels is usually unnecessary, but even a single chapel set in carelessly here and there would break the monotony of the long lines of walls, while the lines would still remain to lead the eye onward to the altar. Besides, as in the old churches, a niche or side chapel of less height than the wall would, by contrast, give the appearance of greater loftiness to the church.

In France and southern Germany, Roman ruins were an inspiration to the artists and taught the use of the round arch and seried columns. The term "Romanesque" is generally applied to these countries because in other lands the artistic and architectural work is divided into specific groups which nevertheless all belong to the general class of Romanesque. We shall therefore, pass to a discussion of those branches of the style which are of special interest at the present time.

The Lombard Style

The Lombard style of northern Italy is widely used for American churches at present. Probably it would be true to say that it is the leading mode of design. Its description, then, is important.

INTERIOR, ST. AGNES CHURCH, CLEVELAND, OHIO

John T. Comes, Architect, Pittsburgh, Pa.

Round arches. Ornament somewhat more profuse than usual in the Romanesque style. This was one of the early churches showing a trend to original treatment.

THE ROMANESQUE STYLE

During the darkest ages permanent stone churches were being built in northern Italy in a style which had developed from the basilica form. Byzantine influence did not extend everywhere. At the same time that the eastern style was being used in some places in Italy, others were developing a style of their own. Many of these churches have not lasted until our day. One of the oldest that remains to us is that of St. Ambrose of Milan. Instead of a flat ceiling it has a round, vaulted ceiling supported by round arches. These, in turn, rest on heavy piers instead of slender columns. It should not be accurate to call it a basilica. It represents a new style of design. The piers are a cluster of columns to suggest the idea that each column, as it leads up to an arch in the ceiling, has its own definite work to do in supporting the roof. It is the beginning of logical construction.

Other Lombardic churches are those of Pavia, Piacenza, and still others in Milan. In the time of Charlemagne, Pavia was a center of scholarship and culture, which probably had an effect on the church building of his day. The Certosa of Pavia, several miles from the city, is a wonderful museum of art. It is of later date but reflects the Lombard style. Few churches of the world present such a storehouse of ornament. The church of St. Francis of Assisi is also an example of structure and ornament.

The Lombards were a Germanic tribe which settled in north Italy. They introduced several new ideas into Italian art. Among these was the use of grotesque beasts representing virtues and vices. That sort of ornament was used also in some of the early Gothic churches. The Lombards rested columns of their doorways on the backs of grotesque lions or other animals. They introduced the recessed doorway, with a series of columns differently carved. This was one way of ornamenting the thick walls of the doorway and was also used in later churches. They further employed the round or wheel-window above the doorway in the façade, or front of the church, and made good use of arcades for

EXTERIOR OF CHAPEL, NAZARETH HALL, PREPARATORY SEMINARY, ST. PAUL, MINN.

Maginnis and Walsh, Architects, Boston, Mass.

Illustrates appropriate use of brick. Geometric lines. Even the brick fence is an important part of the composition. The square tower is more powerful on account of the small windows. It belongs to the chapel but is the axis of the entire group.

ornament. The latter consisted of small arches supported on pillars.

In other parts of Italy more attention was given to mosaics. They were utilized for the decoration of altars, pulpits, spiral columns, and even for outside ornament. The beautiful tower of the Cathedral of Florence owes its rich color combinations to inlaid marble. That sort of ornament, however, did not spread to Western Europe except when done by traveling Italian artists. From the beginning to the present time Italian architecture has been most concerned with surface ornament. Western Europe has always been more interested in form.

The Romanesque churches of France were almost all Benedictine monastic chapels. They were plainer in style than those of Italy. Ornament was crude, owing to the fact that since classical times people had forgotten how to represent nature. The few carved and painted figures of that date lack reality — somewhat after the manner of Byzantine art. They had, however, a decorative value. Later, when great artists appeared, architecture itself declined.

The carved ornament consisted of zigzags and crude motifs from nature. The general effect, however, as beheld from a distant view, was good, inasmuch as the carving relieved the somber grayness of the walls. Painted wall ornament was mostly found in the sanctuary and chapels. All-over patterns in red and black occurred, while columns were striped in red, dark green, and yellow or gold. But the main beauty of the churches was structural.

The Norman style was a branch of the Romanesque. It was brought from northern France to England and also to Sicily and southern Italy. The Normans loved great space and height and to them probably is due the credit for the stately naves of later Gothic churches. They built high ornamental doorways, with a round arch, sometimes reaching to the top of the façade, and

HOLY ROSARY CHURCH, BRIDGEPORT, CONN.

A. J. DePace, Architect, N. Y.

Modern adaptation of the Romanesque style. Practical and low in cost. Massive simplicity, balance, rhythm, and effective ornament. The lack of cornice and the rigid lines of the bell towers show the hardness and directness of granite in logical con-

INTERIOR, HOLY ROSARY CHURCH, BRIDGEPORT, CONN.
Stone walls. Arched colonnade and architraves. In the sanctuary is a painting, representing the title of the church. The interior design has restraint and good taste in structure, furnishings, and decoration.

enriched with the recessed carved columns first used by the Lombards. The entire front was an invitation to enter and adore. The high recessed portal is an important part of the design of the National Shrine now being constructed in Washington.

In all the branches of Romanesque style the tower became an integral part of the building. It was no longer detached, as in the early basilicas, or when merely standing alongside the church. It was built into the structure itself. Sometimes a number of towers were used to add to the beauty of exterior and interior. A suppressed tower, over the crossing of the nave and transept, took the place of the dome in giving light and making a central axis for the church.

Windows were small, lest they might weaken the walls. Stained glass had not yet been invented. The small, round-arched windows were grouped together, giving the same effect as the arcades of the Lombard style. The arcaded cornice became a feature of the style everywhere, and around the cornice, on all sides, was a series of suppressed round arches. Monastery cloisters were inclosed by round-arch arcades which made the monastic group a scene of beauty.

Modern Romanesque

The Romanesque style has commonly been used in America, although without any historical reason. Reversing the natural order, the American pioneers used a classical style, while their descendants preferred the taste of pioneer Europe. In the seventies and eighties of the preceding century a revival of the Romanesque style was started by Richardson and had many followers. Besides churches, many public buildings of those days were erected in the Romanesque style. The windows have round arches. Small, narrow windows are clustered together. Towers are popular. Above the entrance may be seen a great round arch of stone. Except for the stone trimming, the buildings are of red brick or red sandstone. Some beautiful exteriors were constructed in this style but there was no attempt to continue the style in the interior.

A church built in the Romanesque style might be expected to have in its interior two rows of piers, supporting a high central nave, with lower aisles at each side. Instead, we find wide auditoriums, without piers or pillars and without a vaulted ceiling. Perhaps we might consider this an adaptation to our times, but the structure and ornament of the interior is usually in the Italian Renaissance style, showing a misunderstanding of the Romanesque. Many people speak of such a church as built in the Roman style. Romanesque means the opposite of Roman. It was developed outside of Rome but used the round arch of pagan Rome and the Basilican plan of Christian Rome. No such churches were erected in Rome itself.

To be logical, a Romanesque church should have an interior of monastic simplicity. It requires little ornament. We should remember that the original Romanesque style was a pioneer style, crude and unfinished. We may adapt the style to modern construction and taste in ornament, but that is not to be done by combining it with another historic style. There should be harmony between the interior and exterior. The ancient churches were built of stone and their structural principles are those of stone buildings. Today, even when we use stone walls, we rarely build a roof of stone, so our problems are more simple. We are more concerned with the final appearance.

The Lombard branch of the Romanesque movement is more popular at present among American architects. It is a more flexible style than the French or German variety. The arcaded cornice is used and the wheel-window for the front, with a recessed entrance. Its medieval Italian square bell tower is simple but decorative. The style has been adapted to modern conditions and treated as a living style. The proposed tower of the National Shrine had its inspiration in ancient Italian towers, but it has

CHURCH OF THE PRECIOUS BLOOD, LOS ANGELES, CALIF.

Henry Carlton Newton and Robert Dennis Murray, Architects, Los Angeles, Calif.

Lombard style. Concrete construction. Window sashes of precast concrete. Entrance of tufa-stone. All other ornament cast in place, showing capabilities of concrete.

been modernized. The round arches and window grouping are Lombard, but the general design is unlike anything in ancient Lombardy. It is an American design.

Most American churches built in the Lombard style have flat ceilings. The rounded interiors of a generation ago were built of lath and plaster, but that is not good construction. It is mere pretense. There is no need of such flimsy architecture. Let the walls be of the natural shape of the building. If we cannot have round-roof construction let the ceiling be flat. We have not tried concrete for round-roof vaulting. Concrete was used by the ancient Romans for vaults and domes. The concrete forms would present a difficulty but this could be overcome. In the modern churches of Germany there is a great variety in concrete roof construction. Some of them are barrel vaults in concrete. The concrete forms left quarries and octagonal lines in the ceiling to vary the monotony of gray concrete.

There is no longer any need of a narrow central nave, with clerestory and low side aisles. These were based on stone construction which could not span wide spaces. There are ways of spanning any width of nave and we do not attempt to construct roofs of stone for the simple reason that we can do this better with other material. But the round arch is a line of beauty which should not be entirely abandoned. A vaulted ceiling is more beautiful than a flat one. It cannot be used in every parish church, but the better churches will add to their beauty by the use of vaults. A barrel vault can span a wide nave. Even if we abandon pillars, the church should not be a square auditorium. Tradition calls for a long vista ending with the main altar.

American monasteries have made extensive use of the Romanesque style. A cloister surrounded by round-arch arcades gives the effect of seclusion and gives contrast and balance to the building. One reason for the American popularity of the Romanesque style is its suitability to brick construction. We are not concerned with

[61]

the massive piers and heavy arches of the ancients. We need artists rather than structural engineers. Our problems are not those of construction but of arrangement and beauty of design.

Chapter V

THE GOTHIC STYLE

STRICTLY speaking there are, or should be no styles of architecture. Each good structure is different from the rest and cannot be confined to a class. But, loosely speaking, we may group buildings under a style because of certain forms and tendencies. Generalizing very broadly, there are in Western architecture two main groups, the Classical and the Gothic. The classical Greeks sought mathematical perfection. Their roofs were flat. A door on one side was balanced by a door on the opposite side. Everything was according to rule. There was beauty but no development. Finally, there must result from this plan of measured formality, after several generations, a monotonous exactness of line and unrelieved glare of white marble — beautiful but dead. It is true, however, that colors were applied by the ancient Greeks to the stone, particularly in the pediment, although only slight traces of this painting now remain.

The Romans were not so precise in detail, but architecturally they display more imagination. They were empire builders. They wanted room. They raised doorways and ceilings in rounded arches and vaults. They built majestically. Their temples and palaces are classical in line but they contain the idea of variety and growth which developed after a thousand years into the exuberant glory of Gothic cathedrals. In Roman architecture there was no dead monotony. There was variety and possibility of development. It was a living, growing style less perfect than the Greek, but in some ways more inspiring. It had less refined beauty, but more structural inventiveness. Its quality was grandeur rather than beauty. But it also was classical. There was balanced proportion in structure; the round arches were suggestive of the completeness of a circle; and the ornament of Roman buildings was the carved marble of the Greeks and the color combinations of mosaic walls and floors which required long hours of highly skilled labor.

But the Gothic style was less exact in detail. It loved the irregular and the unexpected. Its spirit could not be contained under a flat roof or dome. It soared to unaccustomed heights, with arches pointing upward like the natural archings of the forest. In those marvels of arch there is no limitation of imagination, no holding down to earth, and no dead monotony. There is visible here not merely earthly but heavenly beauty.

Rules of proportion may have been noted later, but they developed by chance. It was a free and untrammeled style, with the abandon of the Crusaders who gave their lives for a cause which was just and noble. In Gothic structure there were no two churches alike; no two windows, doors, or altars identical in form. It despised the precision of antiquity and built with the recklessness of youth, in typical disregard for its canons. Because this style developed in the former provinces of the Roman Empire, it was, as we have seen, called in contempt by the Romans, "the Gothic" (barbarian) style. Yet it was not designed by the descendants of the Goths. The name, which at first was not appropriate, came finally to be universally accepted when the new style won its right to existence and took its place as a successful rival of the classical styles.

Logical Construction

There is another general division of church architecture based on structure. The pre-Christian Romans used a great deal of slave labor in the construction of important buildings. They built of brick, concrete, or rubble, and so both the exterior and interior of the walls required ornament. On the outside there were marble

SAINTE CROIX CATHEDRAL, ORLEANS, FRANCE

Rebuilt from 1278 to 1329 and again in the Seventeenth Century. Not as good an example of Gothic as Rheims, for example, as some of the lines are ornamental and have no structural reason. But the proportions and variety are good. Representative of an age of faith and devotion.

pillars and pilasters and a thin incrustation of marble, which could not be used extensively because the quarries whence it was hewn were too remote to make this material generally feasible for construction. The interior walls had a marble wainscot, while figured ornament was applied to both walls and mosaic floors. Stucco relief on ceilings and walls as well as carved and plastic ornament, was superficial. These features had no relation to construction, but were applied after the work of the builders was completed.

Christian architecture used structural rather than surface ornament, although its full development required a long time. The basilicas continued to use surface ornament in the form of mosaics on interior walls, but the exterior, built of common material, was often given lines of beauty in design. The bell tower was ornamental in outline only, and the interior arrangement of the high central nave, with lower side aisles, was an inspiration for future development of beauty in form.

The Romanesque style was a definite departure from the Roman classical style. The Roman dome and round arch were used, but the walls had no ornament except their natural structural lines. Piers, door jambs, and other structural parts were carved or painted, but there was no marble incrustation of walls. Marble was not easily available, but that was not the only reason for the new manner of design. There had been pagan thinkers in Greece and Rome, but they did not design buildings. All Christians were thinkers. Logic in their creed became a habit of life and quite naturally was applied also in the building art.

Logical construction and ornament were displayed principally in the roof. A stone roof could not be built flat, so the round vault was chosen. No applied ornament was used, but the beauty of the ceiling consisted in the graceful curves of the vaulting ribs.

Yet the round arch contained possibilities of even more perfect development. Sometimes round-vaulted roofs caved in, while the pointed arch was found to be better suited to stone construction. Returning Crusaders told of the beauty of the pointed arch at the same time that builders were discovering its structural utility.

Straight walls and flat roofs required little planning, but once builders began to use reason in construction they did not stop with the discovery of the pointed arch. The vaulted ceiling began to be supported by clustered pillars, each member of the cluster leading to a section of the roof which it supported. Side walls were strengthened by buttresses, which became the actual framework supporting the roof. Every stone in the building had a special work to do and every line of the building was the result of the studied choice of the best form for stone construction. Neither outside nor inside the buildings was there anything superfluous. The medieval builders loved beauty, but not even in that great cause would they add anything that was not a necessary part in the structure. There was no incrustation of marble outside or of mosaic inside the walls. Nothing was artificial. All was as substantial as the Church which it represented.

"Celestial city Jerusalem,
    Blessed vision of peace,
    Reared to the stars in living stones."
— Office for Dedication of a Church.

Gothic architecture is the symbol of a new civilization. Classical formality had been abandoned. It represented a decadent civilization disguised by an appearance of external beauty which covered its unworthiness. But the new Christian civilization was not hypocritical. Its faults were known to the world as well as its virtues. It cared not for pretense. Everything must be logical in religion, in philosophy, and in the place of worship. A better name than Gothic for the style thus inspired is "Christian architecture."

To understand the principles of structure let us consider the steel framework of a new office building. The frame is the real

[67]

© Pub. Photo Serv., N. Y.

ST. MARY'S CATHEDRAL, MILAN, ITALY

Begun in 1386, completed much later. A forest of beauty in carved marble, but showing some of the faults of late Gothic. Plans are being made now for a high spire in harmonious design.

INTERIOR, ST. MARY'S CATHEDRAL, MILAN, ITALY

[69]

building. Walls are added to keep out the weather and to give utility and ornament. The skeleton is welded or bolted together and can be built in any shape, horizontal, perpendicular, or pyramidal, letting the welded or bolted joints take the stress. But suppose the ends were not joined by bolts, or not welded but joined by mortar, or only balanced in position — then the builder must be a remarkably skillful structural engineer. A single mistake in balance would wreck the edifice by its own weight.

That was the problem of the medieval builders. When building in stone to the highest pinnacle, each stone must be balanced in place or the structure will fall of its own weight, like a child's house of blocks.

Because that problem no longer exists, we moderns have difficulty in understanding and appreciating Gothic architecture and above all in using it for modern churches. A generation ago frame churches had pointed-arch windows and false ceiling vaults of lath and plaster. They were supposed to be Gothic churches, but they failed in their purpose. A Gothic church must be built of stone, but even the early stone churches showed an artificial use of the style. Pointed windows and a pointed steeple and a few flowered finials, here and there, outside and inside the church do not make it a Gothic church. That style cannot be achieved by deciding on what ornament to use and then building a structure to which that ornament may be attached. Logic leads the other way. The needs of the congregation must be found and the church built accordingly, with ornament falling into its natural place.

The medieval builders sometimes showed a remarkable carelessness of design. If a side chapel was wanted in a certain place, it was put there regardless of outline. In this humble way the spirit of self-consciousness, rather common in modern churches, was avoided. We would not think of leaving a steeple half built or capitals uncarved. In our anxiety for the general appearance we give the impression of caring more for externals than for substantial construction.

Gothic means also a certain luxury of ornament in carved stone and wood, rich tapestry, painted ornament of dark red, blue, and gold, richly embroidered vestments, and no less wonderful metal work in sacred vessels. It represents the age of chivalry. It is not merely a style of architecture: it is a picture of medieval life when all belonged to one Church, and kings, princes, and wealthy merchants sought the best artists to erect votive offerings. Religion was the most important thing in the lives of the people and in public affairs. And yet numbers and patronage alone could not have produced such results. Saintliness was common and every stroke of the chisel was an act of worship. Masons and artists did their best for God rather than man. They had no thought of twentieth-century tourists.

equality

Beauty was made for God, not people

A building, perfectly balanced in construction, resting on what appeared to be walls of pictured glass (but which were, in fact, carefully calculated supports), was covered outside and inside with carved ornament. There was order in disorder. At first glance one might imagine that in such a wealth of ornament there was no restraint whatever; but a closer study shows a perfection of orderly plan not equaled before or since. Rheims, for example, is a riot of ornament, with every inch of space covered by lacelike carvings, but not a stone is superfluous and not a chisel stroke was made without consideration for the general plan.

The square towers of former times now became pointed spires, which added greatly to the heavenward soaring spirit. Spires reached upward with the abandon of the forest. There was no thought of earth. It was heaven that mattered. The master builder had a general idea of the plan, but the details were left to the individual workman to design as the spirit moved him. Exactness was not required. Even crude carving answered the purpose, as it was a thank offering of children of the forest.

innocence is not exact

The Gothic style was a development of the basilica. We shall not point out the various stages of its progress, as that lies beyond the scope of our work. The Lombard style was an advance beyond the Basilican. The Norman style improved the vaulting system, and in France the Gothic style finally came to its full coördination and beauty. Thence it spread to England, Germany, Spain, and, in a certain measure, to Italy. The Italian taste remained classical, but some Gothic ornament was used in buildings constructed in another style. Great beauty of color was produced in the cathedral of Florence and the palaces of Venice, yet it was not organic but superficial ornament.

Like other styles, Gothic went through the periods of development, perfection, and decline. The period of progress in France was from the middle of the twelfth to the middle of the thirteenth century. The same stages came a little later in other countries. Here, as in other styles, the decline began when the builders became vain and strove for artistic effects. When steeples became too numerous and too high, vaulting ribs more ornamental than practical, and carved ornament more florescent than any natural beauty, decadence had started. Even during this period of decline, however, churches of great beauty were erected, and wood carving and metal work of startling beauty were produced. But the peak of religious fervor and of artistic endeavor had been reached and passed, and now, in the fifteenth and sixteenth centuries, religious disturbances and the introduction of the classical revival brought to an end the glorious Gothic period, the greatest building age since the world began.

Modern Gothic

Many things have changed since those wonderful Gothic structures were erected but no better style of church architecture has been produced. Although neglected until recently, the style is not worn out. It still retains the spark of life. No more important

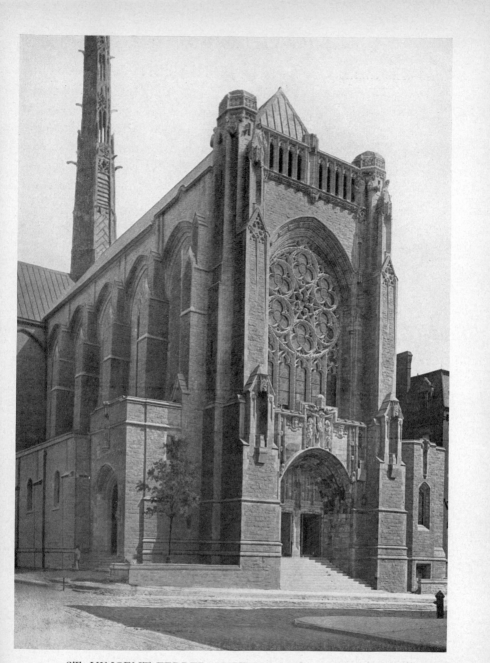

ST. VINCENT FERRER CHURCH, NEW YORK, N. Y.

Goodhue and Anthony, Architects, New York, N. Y.

Showing strength of stone. All lines are based on structural purpose, but
with consideration for beauty of form. No superfluous ornament.

[73]

structural rules have been discovered than the logical distribution of weight and stress, and the designing of a building as one organic whole.

There are no exact rules of measurement for the Gothic style, provided that a reasonable proportion and balance are preserved. The spirit of freedom, however, does not allow us to use forms merely for ornament. Every arch and buttress must have structural use or it is out of place. Attention must be paid to the spirit rather than to the outward form. And inventiveness is just as important now as in ancient times.

No sooner is a new church praised for its design and ornament than immediately imitations of it appear elsewhere. In medieval times nothing was ever copied. There was no repetition of design, although the same master builder would naturally have some similarity in his various conceptions. Yet each capital was different and each pew end was carved with ornaments unlike the others. Originality was considered more important than beauty, for the church edifice was above all a labor of love.

There are two difficulties in the modern understanding and use of Gothic style. One is the change of building material and methods. The other is the spirit of the times.

We no longer, as a rule, build walls of stone, but of brick, with stone used as a veneer. The roof is built of other material and the vaulting problem no longer exists. No unusual skill is required in the construction of a roof, so we do not understand the triumphant success of the past. We see that the final result was beautiful, but failing to understand the structure we cannot understand the ornament. Not wishing to copy a church too closely, we take something from this building and something else from that, finally losing all harmony of design, as the unrelated parts will not fit naturally into their places. Easy, unlabored construction is conducive to meaningless forms and bad style. Gothic con-

INTERIOR, ST. VINCENT FERRER CHURCH, NEW YORK, N. Y.

Goodhue and Anthony, Architects, New York, N. Y.

Majestic arches. Dignity and good proportion. The walls are surfaced
with tile in a warm, cheerful buff color. The altar shown here is temporary.
A permanent altar is now being installed.

ST. PHILIP NERI CHURCH, CHICAGO, ILL.

Joe W. McCarthy, Architect, Chicago, Ill.

Granite with limestone trim. A practical adaptation of the Tudor Gothic style.

struction must have a logical coördination throughout the whole edifice.

Again, this age is different in spirit from the age of the great Gothic builders. It is an efficient, commercial age. We have great engineers and even great artists, but art cannot be a mere community interest. It must come from individual effort. In the Middle Ages the entire community was personally interested in the erection of a new cathedral, helped in the work, and showed an understanding interest in the result. A beautiful church was a sermon to them, and the builders knew that they were leading souls to God.

Many of the great churches were monastery chapels in which the designing, building, and ornamenting were done by monks. If stalls of carved wood were not finished in one generation, still other generations of monks would follow to carry on the work. They need not hurry, for meanwhile they were saving their own souls and helping to save the souls of others by prayer, meditation, and work. But nowadays we have no longer the leisure to spend a hundred years in the completion of a church. Economy leads us to measure the cost; efficiency demands speed in construction, and our practical minds foresee repair bills on steeples and turrets. We therefore leave off the spires and lower the roof, so that the building can be conveniently heated, and we omit the pillars because they would obstruct the view and take up too much space. The result is more useful than beautiful, and yet utility was considered important even by the ancient builders.

A conservative use of the Gothic style, sparing in ornament, tends rather toward the Classical than the Gothic and may in time lead to a new style correct in principle and beautiful in form. But it is not medieval Gothic. We admire the ancient churches, but an age which is negligent in the service of God is not disposed to build a church extravagant in beauty, like a fountain lavishing its wealth and squandering its glory on the four winds of heaven.

INTERIOR, ST. PHILIP NERI CHURCH, CHICAGO, ILL.

Joe W. McCarthy, Architect, Chicago, Ill.

No attempt was made to preserve tradition. A wide nave with flat ceiling in panels. No pillars. Liturgy, acoustics, and seating space given first consideration.

THE GOTHIC STYLE

And here let us give a word of praise to a Gothic form which is rapidly passing out of use — the high steeple. Rising singly over villages, or in groups over cities, it was a constant reminder that the world had not forgotten its Creator. Sometimes the church beneath was not attractive; sometimes it was not even Gothic in form, but the distant view was inspiring. The idea came from the many-spired Gothic, but the single spire became typically American. Our forefathers thus made a noteworthy contribution to external worship if not to art.

Many of the early American attempts at Gothic were failures. The one great exception was St. Patrick's Cathedral of New York. It was designed by James Renwick and the corner stone was laid in 1858. It is in the decorated style of French Gothic in its full development. At the time it was built, Gothic was not well understood, but St. Patrick's was a great church when first erected and continues to be so now, challenging comparison with the many Gothic churches of more recent times.

The Anglican church took the lead in the Gothic revival in the United States and erected churches with beautiful exteriors when beautiful churches were uncommon. Later, Catholics made the mistake of following the Anglican lead. They built churches with beautiful exteriors, but with interiors lacking ornament and cold as uncontrasted stone and brick can be. Now the Gothic style is better understood. It requires rich ornament of color and carving. A church interior of any style should express the joy of devotional life.

One reason why Catholics in America have not followed the Gothic revival and made use of that style, exclusive of other styles, may be the half-formed thought that although Gothic is by origin a Catholic style it no longer has that suggestion. There are, of course, other reasons such as the cost, the distance from stone quarries, lack of stonemasons, and the practical spirit of the time. It is surprising that there should have been a Gothic

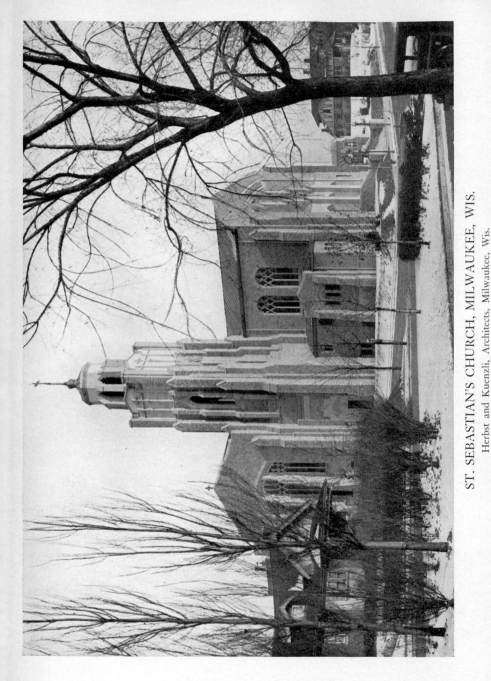

ST. SEBASTIAN'S CHURCH, MILWAUKEE, WIS.

Herbst and Kuenzli, Architects, Milwaukee, Wis.

Many splendid churches have been built recently in the Gothic style. This one is presented as one having good proportion and an interesting design of tower.

revival at all in these unthinking days. A medieval cloistered Gothic group does not represent, for example, the spirit of a modern university.

Progress in Gothic construction was long delayed by talk of English Gothic and thirteenth-century Gothic. We are now starting to build American Gothic. English Gothic was adapted from the Normans and French to suit English taste in ancient times. It produced many beautiful churches and secular buildings, but after four centuries we cannot go back to it as a starting point for an American style. It made use of ornament not based on structure and is therefore not a good model. Tudor Gothic became popular in this country because it allows low wooden ceilings and plain walls and is suited to brick construction. But there is no need of retaining an ancient name. We would do better to develop an original structural plan and call it American Gothic, not through national pride, but to make our contribution to the progress of the building art.

A good example of modification of the Gothic style is the church of St. Philip Neri, in Chicago. The exterior is traditional Gothic, in brown granite. But the interior is a departure from tradition. It has no pillars and no clerestory. The transept is wide to provide great seating space. But the great departure from the past is in the ceiling, which is not vaulted, but flat, with beautifully colored panels. There is little decoration in the church, but what there is brings out by contrast the cream color of the walls. The walls are powerfully built and the structure has a majestic simplicity. It tends toward the classical in spirit and yet we cannot say it is incorrect Gothic. Certainly it is not ancient Gothic; it is American.

Within the past few years a considerable number of Gothic churches have been erected in this country. One of the best of the early churches in this style is the Dominican church of St. Vincent Ferrer, designed by Goodhue and Anthony, and erected in the years 1916–18 in New York. It has a high central nave, simple and austere in line, while the warm colors of the tile surface make the interior an aid to prayer.

Many other Gothic churches have been erected since. They are not copies of ancient churches and do not revel in ornament. They have a somewhat classical restraint and lack pinnacles and niches and wealth of lacelike carving, but they are correct in structure and, best of all, they are our own.

As high, vaulted roofs are beyond the possibility of attainment for ordinary parish churches, consideration might well be given to concrete roofs as used in Germany. Some have ceiling and side walls united in a pointed arch, which springs from the floor. Others have a half-barrel vault, with ornamental ribs. Still others are vaulted somewhat like the ancient Gothic roofs, with ribs in quarries and various other designs. These modern churches will be discussed elsewhere, but here attention should be given to the great possibilities of variety in concrete roofs. Through the use of this material remarkable development could be made in the adaptation of Gothic to modern taste and building conditions.

A few praiseworthy projects in Gothic school and monastic design are Rosary College and the Dominican House of Studies in River Forest, Illinois, a suburb of Chicago; the new building at St. Mary's, Notre Dame, Indiana; and new buildings of St. Benedict College, Atchison, Kansas.

Chapter VI

THE RENAISSANCE

GOTHIC architecture was never fully approved by Italian artists, although in northern Italy use was made of the pointed arch and other Gothic forms. Gothic was the logical development of Romanesque, which originated in Lombardy, but the Italians were unwilling to follow logic to that ultimate conclusion. They never entirely deserted the classical in taste, while the Renaissance brought back the classical to popular favor throughout the world. In former chapters we briefly followed the development of the Roman basilica through various styles of Gothic, beyond which there could be no progress in logical construction. We come now to a style which does not belong to that series. Neither is it a new style in origin. Rome disowned the wayward but beautiful Gothic style and went back to her first love — the classical style of pre-Christian times. The movement became popular throughout the world and even in America the prevailing style, until recently, has been some form of the classical.

The Renaissance was not, as it is sometimes called, the revival of learning. It was the revival of *pagan* learning and *pagan* art. The Church had tried for a thousand years to forget paganism and to blot out its evil influence from the world. In doing so, it had produced a new Christian civilization superior to anything in pagan history. But Petrarch and his followers popularized research into ancient pagan literature and philosophers began to take new interest in Aristotle and Plato. At the same time there sprang up a revival of interest in the ancient classic buildings of Rome and Greece. But before anything new appeared in building design, a new development in painting and mural decoration had already taken place.

BASILICA OF ST. PETER, ROME, ITALY

Architect, Michelangelo Buonarroti

Begun in 1450. The world's largest church. The best monument of the Renaissance style. A great dome raised high above the earth. Truly representative of Rome.

THE RENAISSANCE

Up to the tenth century the Byzantine style prevailed to a great extent, even in the West. Wall decoration was usually in mosaic and in accord with tradition. There was no progress, because features, dress, and colors were prescribed by a definite rule. Neither was there any naturalism, because that was considered pagan. Pictures represented ideas only. They were reminders of Christ, of the saints, and of historical events, but it was thought irreverent to make them lifelike. The colors were symbolic and the color harmony highly ornamental. The mosaic walls of ancient churches have scarcely ever been surpassed in applied beauty. But with the decline of Eastern influence new methods of decoration developed. When mosaic incrustation fell into disuse, painting began to be practised.

The Romanesque style mostly used carved ornament, yet traces have been found on ancient walls, of paintings dating back to the eleventh and twelfth centuries. Cimabue and Giotto were not the first medieval painters, but more is known about their work than about that of the artists who preceded them. Breaking away from the formality of Constantinople, they drew from nature. Their pictures, consequently, although not perfect, had a new animation which foretold great things to come. The walls of the church of St. Francis, in Assisi, were covered by Giotto and his pupils with a series of decorative panels and historical pictures which are of interest, not only because they were among the first of their kind, but also for their real beauty.

During the next two hundred years there lived and worked in Florence, Rome, and other cities the greatest series of mural decorators that history has ever known. We need not mention here the names of all, but among the leaders were Fra Angelico, Botticelli, Sodoma, Perugino, Raphael, and Michelangelo. All studied and copied details of ancient classic painting and sculpture, but they progressed on their own work far beyond their pagan models. If you would see what can be done with colors on a flat surface, study the Grotesques of Raphael and his

© Pub. Photo Serv., N. Y.

CENTRAL NAVE, BASILICA OF ST. PETER, ROME, ITALY

Stunning and grand proportion. Ornament in inlaid marble. At the Papal Altar the celebrant faces the people.

pupils in the Loggie, the three open courts of the Vatican. If you would have a proof that man has a soul, view Michelangelo's fresco of God creating the world, painted on the ceiling of the Sistine Chapel. Art never soared higher. After Raphael and Michelangelo it declined.

The traveler in Italy becomes interested in the development of painting before that of architecture. This wrong emphasis was the great fault of the Renaissance style. It paid more attention to ornament than to structure. Many Italian churches are merely shelters for famous mural paintings. It seems strange that architecture and painting should be rivals but that has often been the case. The best Romanesque, Gothic, and Renaissance churches were built when painting was crude in technique and therefore not overemphasized. Later the perfection of painting and sculpture drew attention away from the structure which was to house them.

While France was building the beautiful Gothic cathedrals, Italian painters were slowly developing realism. The paintings of the thirteenth and fourteenth centuries are not perfect in design, but they delight by their simple sincerity and devotion. At the same time sculptors were creating works of lasting beauty. Painting and sculpture came first, and then structure. Many of the great fresco artists were also architects, but usually ornament was given more importance than structural principles. The logical distribution of weight and stress, by Gothic builders was forgotten or ignored.

Early in the fourteenth century builders began to abandon the Romanesque style in Italy and to imitate the glories of ancient Rome. The various classic orders were revived, but especially the Corinthian. Other Greek ideas were also introduced as they had been used by the ancient Romans. The Greeks, however, preferred horizontal lines and the dominant ideas of Roman builders were the round arch and the dome. The dome had never been abandoned. It had been used to vary the lines and to give light

CHURCH OF SANTA MARIA DELLA SALUTE, VENICE

1631. Showing the success of Renaissance architects in the arrangement of
beautiful views. A church of beauty, although in the Baroque style, which
usually ran to excess.

in the Byzantine and Romanesque styles, but it was now given a new importance. Domes became prominent in the view of Italian cities and took the place of spires in the skyline of the cities of Western Europe.

The Basilican type had always been traditionally Catholic. The long central nave, with clerestory, and the flanking side aisles had been used in all styles up to and including Gothic. But now the structure and form were not considered so important. It was the ornament which mattered. The Basilican form was still used, but the circular and octagonal forms were more popular. Instead of a longitudinal axis a central axis was substituted, with a dome as the center of interest.

St. Peter's in Rome, the greatest achievement in this style, has a dome as its most important feature. It has heavy piers instead of columns and is thus inclined more to the Byzantine than to the Basilican type. In fact, the nave was not planned by Michelangelo to be long as at present. That was a later change of plan. Bramante conceived it as a square church with a central dome. Michelangelo modified that plan, but kept the idea of a central axis. Later on the church was lengthened, but on great occasions the worshipers gathered round the central altar.

To harmonize with new buildings, old buildings were restored in the new style. We know from old pictures that the Vatican palace had been Romanesque, but it was now enlarged and remodeled in the new style. The basilicas built by Constantine, with original deviations from the prevailing style of Rome, were now restored in a less artistic way. Their columns were incased in heavy piers. The walls were covered with wealth of ornament in stucco, paint, and gilding, or incrusted in veined marble of various colors. The outstanding feature of this new style was richness of ornament, and church furnishings themselves were carved in wondrous beauty. In the palaces and other secular buildings, even a greater artistry was displayed than in churches. Palaces and country villas abounded in carved and inlaid furniture which

[89]

rivaled the beauties of nature. Public fountains, statues, grand staircases in parks were all delightful to behold, whether seen at close view or in long vistas.

Then came the decline. Artists became dizzy at the heights of inspiration. They began striving for effect: Ornament grew overelaborate; structure was lost sight of in a maze of restless, voluted decoration; designs were not seldom artificial and frivolous; wealth, material, and fame were wasted in a refinement of meretricious ornamentation, conducive neither to art nor to devotion. From that decline the world never recovered.

We speak of the Baroque as the age of decline, but even such great artists as Raphael and Michelangelo introduced pagan gods and sibyls into their paintings. The argument from the sibyls, it is true, had value in Apostolic times, but paganism was now outdated. Angels had formerly been painted as having human form, with wings to represent spirituality, but in the Renaissance they were pictured as pagan genii and cupids. The two artists mentioned were religious men, but the spirit of the age was represented by its art. The Renaissance left to the world a bad inheritance and an unhallowed memory. Worst of all, it led to the religious discord of the sixteenth century.

But the classical revival was not entirely irreligious. The popes were leading patrons of the Renaissance. Michelangelo was engaged to decorate the Sistine Chapel and Raphael was similarly employed in other parts of the Vatican palace. They were the ablest artists at a time when all artists were great. Both studied pagan ruins, but both were devout Christians. The followers of these gifted masters could not improve on their work, and the decline then set in. Paganism was triumphant at last. Humility and reverence were lost. Too much attention was paid to the copying of ancient models. There was too much formalism. Ancient structures were measured and rules drawn as strictly as those of the Byzantine artists. The classical style was now no longer living but dead.

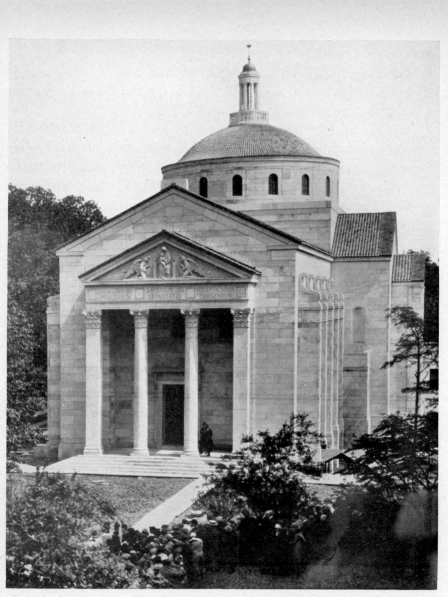

CHAPEL, TRINITY COLLEGE, WASHINGTON, D. C.

Maginnis and Walsh, Architects, Boston, Mass.

A building of classic dignity and power. Restrained in ornament but with sufficient variety of form. Rates highly among modern Renaissance designs.

Art passes from one extreme to another. First it is too formal and then too ornamental. The favored period is that wherein the turn of time brings back the golden mean.

A radical movement now began when the High Renaissance had ended. A reaction against cold formalism set in, and rules were purposely broken. Avoiding static severity, men attempted to give motion to stone by huge scrolls and wriggling ornament. Pediments were broken to make room for a trifling detail.

Even great artists like Bernini carved statues to represent motion. In the Baroque age everything was artificial. Marble was imitated in painted and molded plaster. Pillars were painted on walls. Engaged pillars were used as ornament, that is, short pillars were set into the wall in places where there was nothing to support. Ceilings became painted riots of architectural parts, with undraped pagan cupids climbing pillars and resting on clouds. The designs showed remarkable inventiveness, but little devotion.

An extreme style may remain in vogue for a time and be accepted as proper while popular, but it cannot last, especially in the Church. The Baroque style is best suited to the theater, where the spectator must be confronted by a confusion of gay frivolity for a few minutes while he awaits the rising curtain. The Baroque period also supplied the art galleries of the world with a wealth of ornate furniture and metal work. Painting became inferior, but other decoration was splendid in detail, although overdone in the total plan. That style has been used in this country for churches of the Polish and German people. It is not a national style for either of them but was used by custom.

The better features of the Italian Renaissance spread into other countries, notably France and England, although classic buildings are found in almost every country in the world. Versailles presents us with noteworthy achievements in this style; the same is true of the public buildings in Paris. The Anglican St. Paul's of London is topped by a majestic dome. Indirectly the classical revival spread to North and South America. The Capitol and

ST. JOHN'S CATHEDRAL, MILWAUKEE, WIS.

Victor Schulte, Architect, Milwaukee, Wis.

1847–1853. A good example of the Rococo style. Built for early settlers of South German nationality. This style is usually unrestrained in spirit, but this example has order in variety. Good proportion of gradually receding sections starting from wide base.

CARMELITE CONVENT OF THE INFANT JESUS, SANTA CLARA, CALIF.

Maginnis and Walsh, Architects, Boston, Mass.

Conventual simplicity with beauty suggestive of spiritual joy. An adaptation of the Spanish Renaissance style.

public buildings of Washington are in that style, as are also the most of the state capitols.

Modern Use

Through various revivals and adaptations of the Italian Renaissance some form of the classic style has been used in the design of most American churches. The Basilican outline of the Gothic style, with pillars and a narrow nave, has never been widely popular in America. The Renaissance is a more careless style. The hall form of church may be used without pillars and with little attention to structure. A dome is not necessary, as it was not designed in every case in Italy. In most churches we have had the good taste not to use the false façade of the Baroque style, which has no relation to the church which it fronts.

The Richardsonian Romanesque style was careful about composition, and in our use of the Renaissance style we have been influenced by the Romanesque, owing, in many cases, to our ignorance of the difference between the two styles. But our round-arch style, whatever its general merit, is usually fairly well designed on the exterior. The interiors are not so good. There has been great improvement recently, but many churches still in use have their round-arch ceilings and sanctuary apses molded out of flimsy material. A round ceiling is more beautiful than a flat one, but it should be of sound construction, as a church is not the proper place for pretense.

Many church decorators in the United States make use of the Baroque style, which was outdated long ago. If the architect neglected to put pilasters along the side walls, they cannot later be painted on with propriety. If a parish cannot afford marble pillars, the painting of marble veining on brick and lime plaster piers is a poor substitute. If this device actually deceives the beholder, it is dishonest. If, on the contrary, it is recognized as an imitation, it inspires disgust rather than admiration. The problem might have been solved in other ways with much better effect. A solid color of a pleasing tint would be more satisfactory. Or the space might be paneled with flowered figures, so beautifully treated by the artists of the Italian Renaissance. Or it could be divided by horizontal lines, which would give the effect of a stone pier, without being an imitation of stone. It will be a good thing for American churches when unemployment strikes the "marbleizing" industry.

The theory of Renaissance and Baroque decoration is based on the idea of applied decoration. It is directly opposed to the Gothic plan of ornament, which considered structure all important. The Gothic builders sometimes painted and often carved an arch or door jamb, but first it had a useful purpose and the idea of decoration was secondary. But in Renaissance architecture structure was of little importance in comparison with ornament. A pillar or a wall was a place for applied ornament which need have no connection with structure. Due probably to these fundamental principles the Gothic builders did not introduce such refinement of detail as the classic Italian decorators, but the Gothic churches achieved their purpose better. They aided devotion, while many Italian churches attract visitors as would an art museum, but fail to inspire devotion. In modern church decoration, then, it would seem to be unnecessary to cover every portion of the wall with ornament. It is illogical and therefore to be avoided.

The Renaissance started as a revival of classic simplicity, but it soon abandoned that spirit and became more unruly than the Gothic style, which the Italians considered an outlaw. The late Renaissance was almost as rebellious as the present modernistic art.

The classical style should be represented either by the majestic simplicity of the original or by the dignified lines of the early Renaissance. In the Augustan age the outline of the structure was the important thing. The ornament was secondary. We are far enough away from the pagan age, and the classical style has now

ST. VINCENT'S CHURCH, LOS ANGELES, CALIF.

Albert C. Martin, Architect, Los Angeles, Calif.

Concrete construction in the Spanish Renaissance style. The original examples
lacked proportion, but the modern adaptation used elaborate ornament only as
a contrast to plain wall space.

FAÇADE, CHAPEL OF ST. VINCENT'S ORPHANAGE, SAN FRANCISCO, CALIF.

A modest plan in the Spanish Renaissance style.

been so long used for churches, that there can be no reproach attached to the use of it. It has, we may say, been Christianized.

Excessive formality makes a church interior cold and uninviting, but excess of ornament is worse. Logical construction and restraint in ornament are important, but the main thing needed is the artistic touch. No amount of reasoning can make up for the lack of artistic ability.

The Renaissance started with the intention of reviving the classic spirit, which is the opposite of the Gothic spirit. The former is traditional and conservative. The latter is progressive. But looking back we find that the Renaissance finally broke away from all restraint, while the best Gothic, although inventive, was subject to the dictates of logic and harmony.

The following quotation will tell us what the Renaissance should have been. It is taken from *The Classic Point of View,* by Kenyon Cox (Scribner's Sons, 1911).

"The Classic Spirit is the disinterested search for perfection; it is the love of clearness and reasonableness and self-control; it is, above all, the love of permanence and of continuity. It asks of a work of art, not that it shall be novel or effective, but that it shall be fine and noble. It seeks not merely to express individuality or emotion, but to express disciplined emotion and individuality restrained by law. It strives for the essential rather than the accidental, the eternal rather than the momentary — loves impersonality more than personality, and feels more power in the orderly succession of the hours and the seasons than in the violence of earthquake or of storm. And it loves to steep itself in tradition. It would have each new work connect itself in the mind of him who sees it with all the noble and lovely works of the past, bringing them to his memory and making their beauty and charm a part of the beauty and charm of the work before him. It does not deny originality and individuality — they are as welcome as inevitable. It does not consider tradition as immutable or set rigid bounds to invention. But it desires that each new presentation of truth and beauty shall show us the old truth and the old beauty, seen only from a different angle and colored by a different medium. It wishes to add link by link to the chain of tradition, but it does not wish to break the chain."

That describes the Catholic spirit as well as the Classic spirit. The Classic revival failed to attain the perfection of art achieved in ancient Greece and Rome, and it could scarcely be called a Catholic movement even though favored by some of the popes themselves. But Catholic art through the ages has sought the beauty, the spiritual perfection, and the ever newly interpreted tradition of the past. Adherence to the classical spirit does not prevent the development of new styles. It merely preserves rules which new styles may not break.

American churches in the classic style have more attractive exteriors than many exteriors of the Italian Renaissance. A common feature to be noted in them is the steeple which was introduced by Sir Christopher Wren in London, at the beginning of the eighteenth century. A conical or pyramidal spire tops a square-towered belfry, ornamented by a cluster of pillars in classic design. The idea of a spire came from Gothic architecture, but when treated in the classic style it adds greatly to the churchlike appearance. It became the main feature of American Colonial churches and in them it was very sparing of ornament. It is used in many new churches, which seem at first glance to be Colonial in style, but whose wealth of classic detail shows them to be a modern development of the Renaissance. Not all of them are topped by spires. Some belfries are round and others square, with a flat roof, and still others end in a small dome. There is a great variety in the way in which pillars are used singly or in clusters. At the present time high spires are not popular, but a Renaissance belfry may be low and small, and yet can remain attractive and distinctive. These classic belfries are not common in Italy, but they harmonize well with a church in the Italian Renaissance style.

Chapter VII

MISSION AND COLONIAL STYLES

ALL the styles described in previous chapters had some connection with Rome, either in origin or development. The Gothic style was not used in Rome, but was a development of the Basilican style. It was appropriate that the church which looks to Rome for authority should adopt ideas in church building from the spiritual capital. It was especially fitting since the old styles were better than anyone could or did invent later. There were local diversities, however, in each country, for people differ in taste. When art was at a high stage of excellence more original variations were made. When art declined, originality ceased and builders were satisfied to copy the great works of the past. A description of the development of each of the major styles, with all the numerous national variations, would require an extensive historical work.

The American adaptation of the ancient styles is not a story of great achievement, but during the same period of time the old countries did little better. For four centuries there have been no great artistic achievements anywhere in the world.

Starting out as a new nation, the United States would have done better in architecture if the achievements of Europe had been reasonably relegated. Starting with plain walls and a roof, there would naturally have been a gradual improvement in line and ornament, and possibly there would have been no retrogression. As it was, the structural styles of Europe were copied without understanding. There was no dominant style, and hence the general eclecticism in the choice of architecture ranged abroad as widely as from England on to China and Japan. Since there is no approved Catholic style for churches, nothing hinders a reasonable freedom of choice. Each country is allowed to develop

SAN BUENVENTURA MISSION, VENTURA, CALIF.
Founded 1782. An old Franciscan Mission, showing pioneer humility, simplicity, and devotion. The buttresses suggest permanence. The bell tower has depth, shadow, and gives balance to

a suitable local style of church, adhering, however, to liturgy and tradition.

Either because fresh from Europe and still bearing untarnished in their memories the artistic glories of the past, or because their characters themselves were sturdy and simple, the American pioneers built better than did the men of a later time. Unassuming structures of pioneer days retain a charm of style not attained by many million-dollar edifices of less spiritual times. The same is true of all sections of the country, and of the American territory explored and settled by natives of various nations.

The California Missions are charming in their rugged utility and dignity. They have some of the beauty of nature and seem to have grown up in their setting. In California, New Mexico, Central and South America, the Jesuits and Franciscans built cloistered inclosures for converted Indians. The building was done by the Indians, under the direction of the Fathers, with little or no thought of artistic effect. We may imagine, however, that many a finishing touch was given by a missionary hand. Adobe came from the earth and timbers came from the forest. Everything was plain and unpretentious. The Jesuit Reductions had some ornament of portal and altar in the Baroque style, adapted to pioneer conditions. The Franciscan Missions were more simple, like the convent of the Poor Man of Assisi, with its tables and benches made by monks who were greater as saints than as carpenters. St. Francis would have been entirely at home in an adobe cloister with the children of the wilderness.

Within a square inclosure the monks built a church, a home for themselves and for Indian converts, and the workshops. Adobe was the usual material (although in a few cases stone was used). The furniture was roughly carved with crude implements. Rich ornament was impossible, but sometimes there is an admirably artistic touch in the molding of a doorway, or in the outline of an arcaded cloister, or perhaps in the form of the bell tower. No marble pillars were available for the church. There

THE OLD MISSION, SANTA BARBARA, CALIF.

Fray Antonio Ripoll, O.F.M., Architect

Despising art, the missionaries were great artists. With them honest spirituality came first.

were no painters or stone carvers to decorate the façade or the interior. The material did not call for ornamentation and the people would not have valued it. It was logical, therefore, to build in a plain, simple style, suited to the material, to the men, and to the place. Yet it was not peasant architecture, for it was directed by cultured men. The result, even as still witnessed in the mere ruins of the past, has won the admiration of succeeding generations.

Costly material is not necessary for artistic building. The design and the spirit are more important than the cost. But not every plain building is artistic. Neither is every expensive one. Many churches, built of the best material that money can buy, are lacking in artistic design. On the other hand, many plain buildings do not attain classic simplicity, and an adobe Mission might readily have been gloomy and depressing. But the attraction of these ancient structures is due to their monastic simplicity and sincerity, and to a restrained love of the beautiful in the hearts of their saintly designers. The missionaries brought with them memories of grand churches and dignified cloisters of the old world. A well in the center of the inclosure recalled to them memories of monastery gardens in old Spain and here, in the new world, supplied them with a bit of earthly comfort amid the desert. The outside world was forgotten, as all buildings, including the church, faced the center of the *patio*.

Present-Day Application

Like all other styles of architecture, the Mission style, too, is suggestive of traditions which cling to it. It is a Catholic style, since it has been used by no other church. It is more proper in the South and Southwest and in California, where there are Spanish traditions and where many secular buildings are constructed in the Mission style or in a style which harmonizes with it. It cannot be used indiscriminately as it must have the proper atmosphere.

INTERIOR OF CHAPEL, ST. MARY'S COLLEGE, ST. MARY'S, CALIF.

John J. Donovan, Architect, Berkeley, Calif.

Monastic simplicity gives the proper atmosphere to a scholastic chapel.

CHAPEL, ST. MARY'S COLLEGE, ST. MARY'S, CALIF.

John J. Donovan, Architect, Berkeley, Calif.

This chapel is the climax in a group of buildings of St. Mary's College. All are in the low, simple style of the Missions. The ornament of the chapel is that of the Spanish Renaissance used in the Reductions rather than in the plainer Missions.

[107]

RECTORY AND CHURCH OF THE HOLY SPIRIT, LOS ANGELES, CALIF.

Henry Carlton Newton and Robert Dennis Murray, Architects, Los Angeles, Calif.

Other buildings of the group are only partially seen. A group with simplicity, variety, and balance. Whiteness demands attention and is symbolic in a church group.

A church in that style, surrounded by metropolitan skyscrapers, would seem truly to be "lost in a big city." To create the proper atmosphere there should be an entire group in that style — church, school, and rectory, joined by cloistered walks. The Mission style cannot be given the grand manner. It must remain simple and common, both in material and decoration. If grandeur is the aim, another style should be used. Good material might well be employed — for example, marble for the altar — but a high, ornate altar would contradict the Mission spirit. This style of church has rarely been used with success in modern building, as pioneer simplicity no longer exists. We insist on having everything elaborate.

The Mission style is well suited to monasteries and convents. It is suggestive of the vow of poverty and of retirement from the world. Without copying, use could be made of massive, plain walls of stone or appropriately of concrete. A rough surface in concrete might best resemble adobe. Cover the roof with red Spanish tile to give color and use cloisters to give light, shade, and depth to the design. Instead of building flush with the street, it would be an interesting innovation to have all the parish buildings face an inner square, and then to surround the property with a wall. Even the church itself, instead of opening on the street, might be placed across the court, with its portal facing the entrance gate. On account of its height the church would not be hidden from the street, but this arrangement would give a sense of retirement from worldly distraction. The church of St. Cecilia in Rome has such an entrance court, since Roman dwellings were so arranged and the first churches were patrician homes.

Often the cost of a church is a big problem. With the Mission style the cost may be kept low. The roof is flat, the walls are straight, the belfry is simple, and the furnishings are plain.

By Mission style we have referred to the simple outlines of the

[109]

ST. JAMES CHURCH, MUKWANAGO, WIS.

Brielmaier and Sons Co., Architects, Milwaukee, Wis.

A new building which presents the pioneer spirit of the early Missions. Good balance of plain wall, with contrast of enrichment. The unfinished rock surface is a reminder of rugged pioneer life. The bell niche is distinctive. The entrance is well designed.

Franciscan Missions. The Jesuit Reductions were more ornate, although they too built of adobe in pioneer times. Doorways and fronts were decorated in the Spanish Baroque style, learned in the old country and taught to the Indians. The style is usually called Churrigueresque, after Churriguera, who first used it in Spain. Should it cover an entire building, it would be an excess of ornament, but it was used in contrast to masses of plain wall space, and as such is highly pleasing to the eye. We are not here considering cathedrals in this style as they did not extend north of Mexico.

A few churches and allied buildings have, during recent years, been constructed in this style, and with pleasing results. The graceful curves of the ornament, breaking the dullness of straight lines and white, flat surface, make a composition classical in effect. But the traditions of this style are Spanish, and the ornament is so unusual that the style cannot be used everywhere. The Franciscan Mission style is less ornate and at times could be blended with the landscape in other places than those of Spanish Colonial exploration. The same cannot be said about the style of the Jesuit Reductions. The first impression made by the latter at once takes us back to its Spanish origin, while the ideas first conveyed by the other style are simply Catholic, monastic, and missionary.

A splendid example of group planning in the Mission style is the series of new buildings of St. Mary's College in California, designed by John J. Donovan, architect.

Colonial Churches

Another American development of architecture is known as the Colonial style. It was made popular by Thomas Jefferson, who spent several years in France when the classical Renaissance was at its height. On his return he designed his residence at Monticello and the University of Virginia in that style. It was being used also in England at the same time, a fact which could not fail to have an influence on the colonies.

[111]

During the Queen Anne and the Georgian period, churches, homes, and college buildings in the New World were erected in a modified form of Greek and Roman classic building. The ancients had used marble, but the colonists had to substitute wood. Sometimes, as we might expect, there was a lack of logic in the manner of this substitution of material for forms first used in stone. The training of the designers was imperfect and no artistic ruins were near at hand for accurate study. Yet the sturdy sincerity of the pioneers showed itself in the uncostly but respectable dignity of the architecture they achieved.

Wren had aroused interest in the classical styles by designing St. Paul's in London after that manner. Inigo Jones continued the same method. Later, Gibbs designed St. Martin's-in-the-Fields, in London, with a Greek portico of Corinthian columns. Above the church he placed a pointed steeple, high as a Gothic spire, but decorated in classic detail. The work of Wren had suggested the idea, but the spire erected by Gibb soared higher. From that time on, the pointed steeple became the important feature of churches even in colonial America. For the pillared portico, marble was not attainable, so wooden pillars were cut from the forest and painted white to give the effect of Grecian marble. Our forefathers knew better than to paint wooden pillars with marble veining. There was no desire to deceive. People were poor and of necessity the buildings were plainly furnished. Without striving for effect they thus attained the simple dignity for which the ancient Greek and Roman buildings were admired. Many a Colonial pile of stone has a dignity unknown to more pretentious churches of the prosperous present.

Wood carvers were artists in those days and some of their excellent work appeared in churches of the time, although not to such an extent as in domestic buildings. The spirit of church interiors tended toward simplicity.

It is quite commonly thought that the Colonial style is Protestant, but that is not historically true. The same classical style was used both by Catholics and non-Catholics, but Catholic churches erected before the Revolutionary War were temporary structures. Within a few years after the War many were constructed which still endure. The colonial period was past, but the classical style was used up to the time of the Civil War. The churches of the early Republic began to use brick and stone, rather than wood, and they sometimes lacked the artless nobility of Colonial structures, but the style of design was the same.

The cathedral of St. Augustine, Florida, was built in 1791 to replace an older church. It is in the classic Colonial style, showing both English and Spanish influence. The entrance is Doric, with two columns at each side of the door, supporting a classic entablature. Unlike other churches of the style, the steeple rises at one side and not above the nave. In the usual place of the steeple, the façade is topped by four bell niches in the manner of the Spanish Missions. The bell tower has a square base. Above it are two octagonal sections with a suppressed spire to carry the cross.

The cathedral of Baltimore was planned by the same architect who designed the National Capitol at Washington. It has a dome and transept, and a portico of Doric columns in front. There are two belfries which are small rotundas with domical roofs.

Early in the nineteenth century many other cathedrals were erected in the same style. This was partly due to the influence of Baltimore as the primatial See. But there was no American church style at the time other than the Colonial. The Gothic and Romanesque revivals were to come later. After Baltimore, Colonial cathedrals were erected in Bardstown, Richmond, St. Louis, Nashville, Vincennes, Cincinnati and probably in other cities. Most of them had a portico with a row of pillars. The old cathedral of St. Louis had a square belfry with a six-sided steeple above it. The cathedral of Cincinnati has an octagonal steeple, in seven sections, with engaged columns in alternate sections.

[113]

CATHEDRAL OF THE ASSUMPTION, BALTIMORE, MD.

Benjamin H. Latrobe, Architect

Started in 1803. The architect helped to design the National Capitol in Washington. The Grecian portico is majestic and the cupolas and dome in classic lines give distinction to the roof.

One of the early pioneer cathedrals may still be seen, amid unchanged surroundings, at Bardstown, Kentucky. The See itself was moved to Louisville, but the old cathedral stands back from the road, on the prairie, tall and stately, with a majestic approach. The white pillars of the portico are carved out of the trees felled in the neighboring forest, and the walls of the interior are venerable with paintings donated by royal patrons of brave missionaries. The noble height of the portico and the artistic excellence of the interior, with its many traditions, make it a noteworthy church.

Contemporary Use

And, now, what of the modern use of the Colonial style? In one sense it is an outmoded style, as it belongs to the early history

INTERIOR, ST. JOSEPH'S CATHEDRAL, BARDSTOWN, KY.

John Rogers, Architect, Baltimore, Md.

Shows the nationality of many of the pioneer bishops and priests. It preserves the rich ornament but simple dignity of an earlier age of the French Renaissance

of our country. Yet the various revivals of classical style have, nevertheless, kept that mode popular for a great portion of the Christian era. In every style, Gothic alone excepted, there has been some classical tendency. But each revival has added something of the spirit of its age, and so the Colonial style, in turn, introduced its own variations. It was suited to the time, but colonial conditions no longer exist. It would, therefore, be a backward step to copy the quaint old churches, for it would be an admission that we lack the inventiveness of our forefathers.

The same objection must be raised against copying an Amer-

[115]

ST. JOSEPH'S CATHEDRAL, BARDSTOWN, KY.

John Rogers, Architect, Baltimore, Md.

1816–1819. Truly representative of the colonial spirit. The pillars of wood were cut from the neighboring forest. Until recently no more noble churches were erected in America.

[116]

ican style as against the unthinking use of any other form of architecture. The colonists used the style which for them was logical, at a time when they transplanted the culture of the Old World to the New. But each age must make its own contribution. Those who admire the classical manner should use it in a new way. And yet the Colonial steeple is such a fitting ornament, it cannot well be left unused. Probably it is more logical than a great bell tower, rising from the ground with more strength and greater dimensions than are necessary to support a single bell. On the other hand, Colonial steeples, too, may err, as is the case at times, in not having a visible support. The design would be better coördinated if the support of the steeple started from the foundation. An engaged base would answer the purpose of logical construction.

Some modern churches have used the Colonial steeple, but the rest of the church is designed in accord with present-day taste and with consideration for the material used. That is a logical development of the Colonial style, and in such a church the decoration may be more elaborate than in the pioneer churches. As long as the structure and ornament are classical in spirit there is no obligation to adhere strictly to the Colonial style or to the Italian Renaissance or even to the ancient Greek and Roman. It is an American interpretation of the classical style.

Chapter VIII

ALTARS IN ARCHITECTURE AND LITURGY

THE first Christian altar was a table in the Upper Room in Jerusalem. Probably a wooden table was used for some time after the ascension of our Lord, as Mass was said in private homes and in caves and prisons during three centuries of persecution. Then a wooden chest was made available and Mass was said upon the lid. The altar used by St. Peter in the home of Senator Pudens, and now preserved in the Lateran Basilica, is a wooden altar.

The underground cemeteries, known later as catacombs, were not regular places of worship except in times of severe persecution. Wooden altars were used even there. But on the anniversary of a martyr Mass was said over his tomb, on the stone slab resting upon it. This formed a ready-made altar, and the idea was approved and finally became mandatory. After the persecutions ended, bodies of the martyrs were brought into the city of Rome and placed beneath the main altars of churches. Altars themselves were designed in the form of tombs. Elsewhere, in place of the bodies of martyrs, which were not present there, relics of the martyrs were inclosed in the altar. For several centuries wooden altars were sometimes employed, although stone altars were considered more appropriate. Above the altar in early times was a ciborium of four columns and a cupola, from which was suspended a dove or other fixture for the reservation of the Blessed Sacrament.

For a long time the altar top was unobstructed, like a table. The reredos, the structure at the rear on which candles and flowers are placed, came into use to provide a place for the display of relics of saints. One of the oldest of these is the gold and jeweled reredos of St. Mark's Cathedral of Venice, dating from the tenth century. It was first an antependium for the front and was later placed above the altar table to the rear.

Gothic churches of the fourteenth and fifteenth centuries had high, ornate altar screens, in keeping with the vertical structure of the building. Renaissance churches continued the high reredos in the new mode of design. Baroque churches found it a convenient place to load statues, reliquaries, and vases. And so, down to the present time, we have continued these top-heavy altars which have lost all resemblance to, and all symbolism of, the table of the Last Supper.

American churches are not so high nor so ornate as those of the thirteenth century, but we, nevertheless, continue to use the same high reredos, built out of less worthy material and less noble in design. We have imitated marble with wood in jig-saw Gothic. Many hand-carved wooden altars of Europe are true works of art, but most of our American wooden altars have neither good design nor good workmanship. They are all similar in pattern and have been carved by machinery. With their material left undisguised they would at least be honest, but painted and veined in imitation of marble they have lost even that virtue. The same stricture does not apply to wooden altars painted plain white, since this procedure has been the custom for so long a time that everyone recognizes such an altar for what it is.

Prompted by a new understanding of living architecture, we are for the first time asking the question, "Why?" regarding the forms we select. An old form need not be continued unless it adds beauty to the church. In the case of the high, ornate reredos there was no beauty to recommend its use. We merely continued thoughtlessly that to which we were accustomed. We had forgotten its origin and failed to give proper emphasis to the altar table or to keep the altar screen in the proper background. Very recently, a great improvement has been made in altar designing by making the reredos lower and plainer and by paying close attention to the balance of structure and ornament. We desire to have ornament in the church, but not unguided ornament.

Ordinarily there is no need for a high reredos, unless it be in the form of a canopy. It is quite probable that at first it was intended as an artistic modification of the canopy, but it soon lost all such significance. Usually, however, it has a small canopy extending over the tabernacle and others above statues.

In a well-designed altar the canopy over the tabernacle will be prominent enough that it may not be lost in a maze of ornament. Its purpose is to draw the attention to the tabernacle which is the center of interest in the church. Now that the aim is toward logical construction, the reredos should be either in the form of a canopy or else it should constitute a simple background. It should have no more than its proper emphasis. Evidently the table is more important than the background and this should be emphasized by color, structure, and ornament.

Instead of the reredos of marble or wood, in case the altar be attached to the wall or near it, the altar screen may be a painting or tapestry or a dossal, to be changed with other altar ornaments according to the color of the day or season. The dossal need not be limited in color and design to a repetition of the kind frequently used in this country. Stripes are not necessary unless desired for contrast and to break up a wide space. The use of embroidered emblems on a plain background would give an opportunity for great variety.

A painting makes an appropriate altarpiece. The main altar is dedicated under the same title as the church and might well have above it a painting of the saint or mystery to which it is dedicated. We have been satisfied heretofore with copies of the masters. A demand for original paintings would be a great step forward. It would give individuality to each church and encourage the development of artists. All other arts have been imitated by machinery and therefore cheapened, but painting must be done by hand. It remains the one great field of creative art. Many European churches have as their claim to distinction the possession of a single great picture. Such a friendly rivalry in modern churches would aid devotion and add to the general interest in churches.

A canopy is required over the altar by the *Ceremoniale Episcoporum,* but this ancient rule has become practically obsolete by nonobservance. Yet logical construction requires that the altar be the center of interest and a canopy will best give that effect. The canopy may hang from the wall on chains, to be let down for change of color, or be suspended from the ceiling, or attached to the reredos. It should cover the predella where the priest stands. It may rest on four pillars, as the baldachino in the Lombard and Renaissance styles, and be of stone, bronze, or wood. But we need not be archeological. An ancient style may be modified to suit our particular problem. Even in Rome not every main altar has a canopy. It seems to be required more for artistic than for liturgical reasons.

For a church of importance the baldachino is the most dignified form of canopy. It harmonizes well with any type of architecture, as its four pillars give an opportunity for good structural lines in the interior, where, in American churches, pillars are usually excluded. It further centers attention on the altar, as is proper. An innovation might be introduced into American Gothic by the use of such a canopy designed in Gothic style. It would have more depth and distinction than the flat reredos. There are a few rare examples of such Gothic canopies. Although belonging to another style, the idea might be adopted and harmonized with any style.

And, now, a few words about the kind of altar for each style of church. The basilica represents the Apostolic Church. Early altars were merely tables. Some stone altars were tables resting

ALTAR OF ST. ANSELM'S CHURCH, NEW YORK, N. Y.

Gustave E. Steinback, Architect, New York, N. Y.

Byzantine-Romanesque style. A similar sort of canopy was used above the
main altar in most Italian churches of various styles of architecture. The
canopy is more appropriate than the flat reredos of some Gothic churches.
Where the altar is sufficiently prominent, the omission of the canopy is
tolerated.

on four legs and others had a single leg supporting the center. Others were a solid block of marble. The tomb design is only for those churches which possess the remains of a saint or martyr. At early altars the priest said Mass facing the people, so there could be nothing to obstruct the view. A single gradine for candles avoids the necessity of placing them on the altar table. The basilicas built by Constantine had canopies supported on four columns. The basilica of the Holy Savior, later St. John Lateran, had a silver canopy supported by marble or porphyry columns. On the altar screen were figures of Christ and the Apostles. The basilica of St. Paul has a small canopy with its pillars at the corners of the altar and a larger one to correspond with the size of the church.

The canopy, or ciborium, of many of the ancient churches in Italy is in the Lombard or Pisan style, or some other variation of the Romanesque style. It ends in a shallow dome, square, round or octagonal, with a cupola at the top and a pillared arcade around the lower edge. The use of small pillars is a reminder of the Pisan style. Some variation of this style of canopy was used in Basilican, Byzantine, and Romanesque churches with variations corresponding to the style of decoration.

In the Gothic style the reredos was a variation of the canopy, and its origin was often forgotten. In the better examples the reredos preserved some semblance of a canopy. In earlier times there were curtains around the ciborium, which were drawn at certain times during the Mass. This custom discontinued, curtains were used at each side of the altar, with a dossal, or dorsal at the rear, a curtain of linen, silk, or gold cloth. That sort of altar curtain is now quite commonly used in America. Usually these cloth hangings are changed to correspond in color to the day or season of the Church calendar.

To correspond with the architecture some Gothic churches had an altar screen of marble or wood built high in the air and at-

ALTAR OF THE CHAPEL AT NAZARETH HALL, ST. PAUL, MINN.

Maginnis and Walsh, Architects, Boston, Mass.

A simple style of canopy, adding greatly to the importance of the altar. The entire sanctuary, with its rich background of marble, is perfect in proportion.

tracting attention away from the altar table. In that case the architects forgot the liturgical purpose of the church.

In the Italian Renaissance the canopy on four columns was revived. The dome on the top was designed to harmonize with the plan of the church. In the decadence it became like the rest of the church, too ornamental to be in good taste. Other Renaissance altars, instead of the canopy on columns, have a reredos with pillars, round arches, and ornament according to the style.

A great deal has been written and said about liturgical altars and the rules are simple, yet new altars are being installed without observance of the rules. But now makers of altars are giving attention to liturgical requirements and can furnish properly designed altars when these are demanded.

The following paragraphs are based on decisions of the Congregation of Rites as quoted by Van Der Stappen in *Sacra Liturgia*. The tabernacle should be free all around, so that a curtain may be draped over it. It does not suffice to hang at the front of the tabernacle only, it must cover all sides. The top may be round or conical, so that the curtain may be gathered round it and hang from it. A flat top is not mentioned, but custom seems to allow it.

The Benediction throne should be to the rear of the tabernacle and higher than the top of it. It must have a base, a rear curtain or more substantial screen of wood, metal, or marble, and there must be a canopy. The base alone, on which the monstrance is placed does not suffice. As the throne is used only for Exposition of the Blessed Sacrament, it may be removable and placed on the altar only when needed. If removable, it may hide the cross, since the cross need not be visible during Exposition of the Blessed Sacrament, but only during Mass. The throne is more properly placed to the rear of the tabernacle. If permanent, it may not be above the tabernacle, but if removable it may be placed there during Exposition provided there is no room in the rear.

ALTAR OF THE CHAPEL IN NEW ROCHELLE COLLEGE,
NEW ROCHELLE, N. Y.

This altar follows the liturgical requirement of separate bases for tabernacle, crucifix and Benediction throne. The tabernacle is circular and rests on the table of the altar. It was covered with a veil and an antependium was placed in front of the altar but here we are concerned with architecture. There is only one gradine on which the candles rest with the crucifix in the center. Back of the crucifix is the Benediction throne with canopy. It is used only for Benediction. A larger canopy hangs from the ceiling. The reredos is Gothic but the altar proper is an example for use in any church.

But the most important liturgical rule concerning altars is that regarding the location of the crucifix, as it brings up the question of worship. The proper place for the crucifix is to the rear of the throne and above it. If necessary, the crucifix may be placed on the top of the tabernacle, but not on the throne, as the same honor may not be given to the crucifix that is given to the Blessed Sacrament. To avoid this impropriety in an altar already installed the crucifix could be placed on a bracket or pedestal to the rear of the throne, rather than on the base, which is to be reserved for the Blessed Sacrament. In some cases it is suspended from the reredos and hangs a little higher than the tabernacle and to the rear. That leaves an easier problem of arranging the Benediction throne and tabernacle in separate places.

Some liturgical laws are more important than others. Father Augustine, O.S.B., in *Liturgical Law* (Herder), recognizes a distinction between laws binding in conscience and others which are only directive. He states also that, in liturgy as in common law, an opposite custom of long standing abrogates a law.

Liturgy may be confusing to an architect. One pastor will insist on having what another pastor considers of little importance. Some practices concerning furnishing are adopted by students of liturgy as their own interpretation of what is proper although possibly not required by law. Recently there has been a realization of previous neglect of this sacred science and that is the reason for usages considered new which may be indeed very old. Hence, fixed rules are not given here. It is a matter for interpretation and consultation.

Chapter IX

SMALL CHURCHES

SMALL churches are most likely to be poorly planned, as the best architects are not hired for them. Many small churches are too pretentious. They are planned as cathedrals reduced in size. We must have some beautiful and ornate churches, the best that the age can build, but it is not necessary that every parish church should be a cathedral in size, style, and cost.

It is impossible to give, in a general way, figures which will apply to the size and cost of any proposed church. The cost will vary with the material used and the distance from the source of supply. No two churches are alike, or at least should be alike, in plan. A few figures are given as a standard of comparison to determine the size and seating capacity.

The floor space occupied by each person usually is figured at 18 by 32 inches. Let us start with a row of pews across the church. A 12-foot pew will seat 8 persons. Two will seat 16. Allowing 5 feet for the middle aisle and 3 feet for each side aisle we would have a width from wall to wall of 35 feet or 36 feet, including the walls. The usual space from pew to pew is 32 inches. With 16 people to the row, if we wish to seat 300 people, the length should be 18 pews occupying 48 feet of floor space. To seat 100 more add 6 rows of pews, taking 16 feet of length of the church. There must be a 6-foot aisle at the rear and the same at the Communion railing. The sanctuary should be at least 18 feet deep. Thus we would have a length of 94 feet and a width of 36 feet to seat 400 people.

The same width of aisles and depth of sanctuary are required in the smallest church, so that the addition of more seating space would be proportionately small in cost. In a very small church the sanctuary and aisle would take up half the floor space. As more seats are added the proportion of space not occupied by seats rapidly declines. Therefore it should be poor economy to build any church the actual size for a certain seating capacity. A few rows of seats should be added to provide for possible growth and to take care of visitors on special occasions.

Figures on the comparative cost of building material, given in books of estimates, are based on so many contingencies that to quote them here would be of little assistance. Concrete is more economical for a large church with wide roof span, but for a small church brick walls and timbered roof would cost less.

Fireproof construction, with its lower insurance rate and ending of worry, is worth consideration.

It is well also to provide ahead of time for new developments in heating and air conditioning, which may come within a few years. Well-insulated walls and ceiling will make the use of new methods possible, while a neglect of insulation would make them prohibitive.

The present system of lighting is to let the light fixtures be seen. Indirect lighting threw the light in wrong directions. In a church, light is wanted on the prayer books rather than on the ceiling. The logical plan of church lighting is to have the fixtures above the heads of the people to avoid the glare. Interesting effects are being produced in stage lighting and in advertising, but not every new method is appropriate in the church. Nothing theatrical is desired. But flood lights on the altar from an invisible source will prevent the need of facing bright lights.

Rules on the use of electric lights in churches were quoted by *The Acolyte* of July 9, 1932, from an article in *The Clergy Review* of May, 1932. The Apostolic Visitor of the city of Rome, Cardinal Marchetti Selvaggiani, interpreted the decrees of the Sacred Congregation of Rites in new rules made obligatory in the city of Rome.

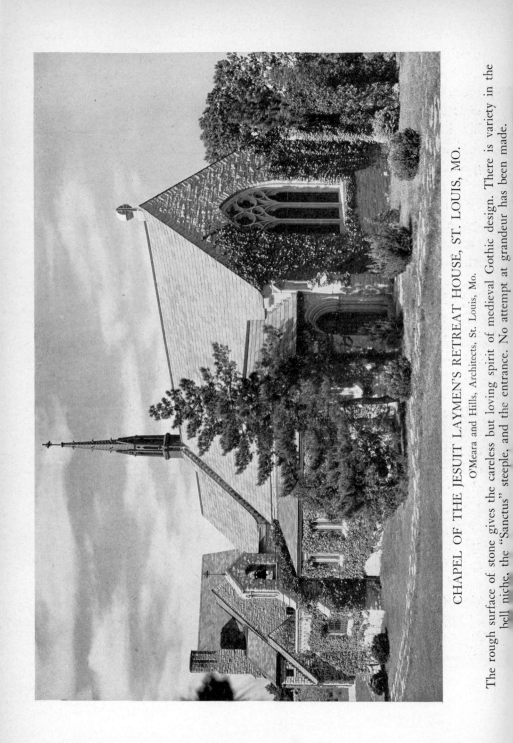

CHAPEL OF THE JESUIT LAYMEN'S RETREAT HOUSE, ST. LOUIS, MO.

O'Meara and Hills, Architects, St. Louis, Mo.

The rough surface of stone gives the careless but loving spirit of medieval Gothic design. There is variety in the bell niche, the "Sanctus" steeple, and the entrance. No attempt at grandeur has been made.

INTERIOR, CHAPEL OF THE JESUIT LAYMEN'S RETREAT HOUSE, ST. LOUIS, MO.

O'Meara and Hills, Architects, St. Louis, Mo.

Walls of Mankato, Minnesota, marble. The altar of the same material is simply carved in a way appropriate to marble. The tabernacle is set in the wall above the altar as was sometimes done in near-Apostolic days. The ceiling is unpainted. There is no striving for effects. The charm of the interior comes from the excellence of material, simplicity of treatment, and the warm color of stone walls.

INTERIOR, CHAPEL OF OUR LADY OF THE ASSUMPTION, ST. JOSEPH'S HOSPITAL, ORANGE, CALIF. Designed by Mother M. Francis, Superior General of the Sisters of St. Joseph of Orange

A pleasing use of the Rococo style of the late Italian Renaissance. In the original style every square foot of surface was covered with undignified ornament. In this chapel there is a background of repose and the gay lines of ornament suggest the spiritual joy of nuns at prayer. The low ceiling of an inclosed chapel is here well treated as a rounded ceiling without painted ornament and bright in tone to avoid attracting attention and thus suggest greater height.

ENTRANCE, ST. ANTHONY'S CHURCH, GARDENA, CALIF.

Henry Carlton Newton and Robert Dennis Murray, Architects, Los Angeles, Calif.

Distinction without great cost. Ornamental detail in precast concrete. The tile over the door is in dark blue, yellow, and yellow-green colors. The cross is of gold-colored tile.

INTERIOR OF CHAPEL, ST. CLOUD'S HOSPITAL, ST. CLOUD, MINN.

Schmidt, Garden and Erikson, Architects, Chicago, Ill.

Showing the strength of masonry with rectangular lines in modern treatment. Relief from severity is obtained by the color and texture of the walls and by the furnishing not completed in the picture.

There are two general rules. Electric light is forbidden (1) as a substitute for the wax candles prescribed at the altar or (2) with a view to producing theatrical effects.

Under the first rule electric light is absolutely forbidden on the altar or in front of and around the exposition throne. The light must come from a fixture separate from the altar.

Under the second rule, electric lights are forbidden for tracing architectural lines or outlining garlands, monograms, etc., and in an unnecessary amount before pictures. The latter may be softly illuminated by light from a hidden source.

But probably the most important rule is that which expresses a preference for lighting a church by electric light "from hidden sources." "On occasions of greater solemnity" standards, brackets, and chandeliers may be used "provided that their direction and position be determined in a manner perfectly corresponding to the artistic requirements, the nobility of sacred edifices, and the dignity of sacred worship."

The point of view seems to be that electric light is not to be used for its own sake as a means of decoration but only to give necessary light. Sentimentality and frivolity are discouraged.

By inference, the rule is opposed to indirect lighting, in which light is thrown on the walls rather than on prayer books, and it favors the latest system of lighting from hidden sources.

As a reversion from indirect lighting architects of churches especially started giving importance to hanging fixtures in the general design, with the idea that the source of light should be seen, but the interpretation quoted above makes the church building more important and the light fixtures less important and less worthy of special attention. Decorative effects by colored lights also are opposed to the intention of the rule, although not mentioned.

The least costly type of construction is the flat roof. It is most appropriate in the Renaissance or other version of the classical

INTERIOR OF CHAPEL, DePAUL HOSPITAL, ST. LOUIS, MO.

O'Meara and Hills, Architects, St. Louis, Mo.

Basilican in plan with Byzantine-Romanesque ornament treated in modern manner. An example of restraint and balance in decoration. An elaborate style treated with the two to three classical proportion. It shows the excellence of contemporary taste in the treatment of any traditional style in a new way. The heavily shaded ceiling is given visual support by strong colors on the side walls. The hospital to which this chapel belongs has been given high praise for artistic design.

style, as for example, the Colonial. It could be used in the Spanish Mission style, in which a timbered ceiling would be quite appropriate. No steeple is required in that style, but only a niche, or open belfry. Those who have used an adaptation of the Mission style have made it too refined. It requires the rough simplicity of pioneer life.

Even a low-priced church should have some variety of line, as straight lines are monotonous. A niche in the wall for a statue, or a side chapel attached carelessly anywhere, will give relief from mechanical exactness.

Money paid to a good architect is well spent. The difference between four square walls and a well-designed church will give a satisfaction beyond all price and will be a more worthy offering to God. Let us imagine a poorly designed church. The door is in the exact center. Above it is a conventional stained-glass window. The bell tower has windows in pairs, rectangular and regularly placed. The top of the tower is battlemented that the parishioners may use it as a stronghold from which to shoot their arrows. The entire building is common and cheap, however large the sum of money expended upon it. An architect of ability would have grouped the windows to show the strength of the tower, would have made the tower parapet less military and more expressive of the material used, would have made the entrance more than an ordinary door, and so the church, although small, would have been inviting. The cost could have remained the same, but the entire edifice would now rise as a worthy sacrificial offering, not of wealth, but of prayerful, worshipful, and intelligent thought.

Permanence of material is important even in a small church. If economy is necessary it may be gained by a low roof and simplicity of outline and ornament. A church of wood is rarely worthy of its purpose unless better cannot be afforded. Brick or concrete cost little more and are more lasting and representative.

ALTAR, CHAPEL, PIO NONO HIGH SCHOOL, ST. FRANCIS, WIS.
In this plain chapel, distinction is attained by altars, statues, and Communion
railing hand carved in wood in special designs.

[138]

SMALL CHURCHES

Stone churches, built in pioneer days by members of the congregation who quarried and laid the stones, are attractive even without variety of design.

Furnishings, too, may be devotional without being costly. An inartistic altar of marble might be a distraction from prayer but even a small missionary church has no excuse for bad taste. A plain wooden altar may be draped with a frontal and tabernacle veil in liturgical colors to inspire devotion by showing reverence for God's presence.

Small churches may reduce cost by not including a choir loft in the plan. In the chapel of the Jesuit Retreat pictured on page 131 there is no choir loft. The organ rests on the floor at the rear of the chapel. It is true there is no regular choir for that chapel, but in a small church the voices of the choir would carry well enough without a special elevation of floor.

In the Holy Child Jesus Church in Brooklyn, there is no choir loft but only a platform three feet in height, between the entrance doors.

Chapter X

INTERIOR DECORATION

SINCE the present volume is concerned not with the writing of history, but rather with the practical problems of modern church building, it will be well to call attention at once to the subject of this chapter as in reality the most important under consideration here. The decoration of churches is of all church-art problems the farthest from being solved. Architects and builders, with some few exceptions, are designing and erecting good structures, but when the building is turned over by the contractor the deface-ment begins. The saddest feature is that all this work is done under the pretense of art.

At one time the more important and costly churches were often made ridiculous by a style of mural painting which was a distrac-tion rather than an attraction. Such abuses are less common now, but many defects remain to be remedied. And here let the reader understand that the principles enunciated in this chapter are in-tended not for decorators only, but for all who are interested in better churches.

Mr. Ralph Adams Cram has somewhere said that since no good decorators are available in America, it were better to leave the walls plain. And yet it is perfectly true that American dec-orators are doing splendid work in homes and public buildings and there is consequently no reason why they cannot do good work in churches as well, provided only that they know what is proper. The main fault is that in church decoration they have been following worn-out styles.

"By decoration is meant the adornment or embellishment of an object by purposed modifications of its form or color." Such is the definition given in the *History of Ornament* by Hamlin.

The modification of form is the work of an architect. Carving or any other relief ornament is added while the structure is being erected. But here we are considering only the modification of color by mural decoration.

One may infer, from the definition, that the adornment is secondary in importance to the object adorned. The form is more important than its modification. The purpose of decoration is to make the form more beautiful — not to center all attention on the ornament.

In a church, therefore, the work of the builder is more important than that of the decorator. The wall mass and outlines are more important than the wall embellishment. This thought will help decorators to practice restraint. A wall is not to be hidden by ornament, but to be made more beautiful. If that effect is not obtained by painting, it would be better to leave the wall in its original condition. It would then be, at least, an honest wall.

Decorators speak of emphasizing the architectural lines. That is the work of architects — not of decorators. If good lines are there, they need no emphasis. If the lines are not good, no amount of painting can improve them. We often see a Gothic ceiling with well-formed arches spoiled by a frivolous, irregular border on the edge of every vault. A border of straight lines might be endured, but the irregular wavings have broken up the only lines of beauty in the ceiling. The architecture has been emphasized by taking away its outline, which is its very soul. Yet no matter what the style of architecture, most decorators will paint along the architectural lines a scroll of irregularly lined borders. If the church were left unpainted, it would have the beauty of well-balanced wall masses and graceful outlines. Take those away and the case is hopeless.

The custom here described probably started in imitation of carved ornament in the great Gothic churches of the past, but carving and painting are two different mediums. Their rules cannot be identical. When a stone rib was decorated by carving (which rarely happened) the outline of the vault was not broken up by irregular lines and the carving was secondary to the general outline.

A precedent for painting might possibly be sought for in the church of St. Francis of Assisi, frescoed by Giotto and his pupils in the thirteenth century, where each panel of ceiling and walls is surrounded by a border. In this instance each border is a frame for the picture within and is not intended primarily to emphasize the lines of architecture. In that case the decorator was more important than the architect. If we had mural painters at the present time with the ability of Giotto, we would tolerate the ignoring of architectural lines and tell them to paint what and where they pleased. Then the world might come to admire, not a great church, but a great painting. That was done throughout Italy during the Renaissance, and for that very reason the Italians have always been better decorators than architects.

Structure versus Ornament

We have here the age-long rivalry between builders and decorators. The great masters of the Renaissance considered a church wall as a canvas spread out to be beautified by their brush. The Gothic builders, on the contrary, regarded a wall as an integral part of a coördinated plan. The wall must be designed to support the roof in an effortless way and be an organic part of a vision of beauty. Pictures were needed somewhere in the church for devotion, but they must be placed where they would not break architectural lines and, like everything else, they must fit in with the general plan.

This question is of such consequence that we must take sides on it before adopting any theory on church decoration. We must decide whether structure is more important than applied ornament. One is not exclusive of the other. All structure must have ornament. But it is a question of relative importance. It is Rome opposed by the provinces. The Romans, including all Italy, built walls of rubble and incased them in thin slabs of marble or richly colored mosaic or pictures by the masters. The Gothic builders used stone undisguised. A single stone was not beautiful in itself, yet as part of a great cathedral it contributed not only to beauty but to strength and unity. We do not deny the beauty of Italian walls, but from the standpoint of logic the so-called Goths had the better of it.

The choice of Roman and Goth between the contrasted styles here indicated has been attributed to the difference of climate. The northern nations, we are told, needed abundance of light and so welcomed the spacious windows of the Gothic, while the Romans, in a country of superabounding sunshine, preferred the shade and coolness of the large wall spaces. This, however, fully harmonized in any case with their natural love for painted presentation.

If, now, the lines of the interior should be left to the architect, the decorator should have a general knowledge of the meaning of those lines, or in other words, should understand the various styles of architecture. Few decorators mix styles of decoration, but many of them have but one style of painting for all styles of buildings. Decorators trained in Italy paint Gothic pointed arches and Romanesque round arches alike in the decadent Baroque style which is of doubtful beauty or correctness in any church. The use of that lawless style is the explanation of so much bad decoration. In past ages, when the Baroque was popular, it was the logical method of decoration. Even a traveler in Italy sees so much of that style, he might be inclined to think it still popular, but it is a national style and not appropriate in America, in other types of churches. The fault is not with the artist's drawing ability, but with the style of art chosen for guiding principles.

German decorators bring to this country their own national interpretation of the Baroque and the New Art style of the 1890's. There are no churches of either type being built now, so there is no place for those styles of decoration.

The Baroque style is artificial. It uses an imitation of architecture — vaults, pillars, etc., painted on flat surfaces, and curtains painted on the sanctuary walls. Such artificial work reminds one of show-window architecture, made to last for a day and then to be destroyed.

We have given too much importance to church decoration. Some painted ornament is needed and some color on the walls, and that will suffice. Such a suggestion will not put decorators out of work, as the coloring must be done by experts. But stencil work is too easy and too mechanical to demand high valuation. The wall was built laboriously and will be admired more for its own excellence than for any facile decoration.

The Use of Color

The lines of painted ornament are very important, but color is even more important, as practically everyone has a sense of color, although many cannot estimate the value of artistic lines. One theory of the pleasure given by color is that certain fibers in the optic nerve are sensible to certain colors. Therefore the sight of a combination of colors gives general satisfaction, while one color would tire the eye. At any rate, our pleasure in beholding color combinations is based partly on cultivated taste and largely on the physical nature of the eye and on natural laws of light. We know from experience that we are pleased by a happy combination of colors. We dislike the monotony of one color and desire variety, but that variety must be harmonious. Both extremes — too little or too much color — are bad.

There are several theories of color harmony. The more commonly accepted one is that every combination of colors should have in it the three primary colors — red, blue, and yellow — in some of their tints or shades. It is not many years since we sought monotony in color, and churches as well as private homes were painted in three shades of green or in dead gray. But modern art, with all its faults, has taught us a new love of color. If a neutral tint or shade is used as a background, high lights of strong color are used here and there to enliven the general effect.

People once turned against colors because they had been used without harmony. The various colors were given equal prominence and the result was quarrelsome. A later improvement was the use of a pleasing neutral color for large spaces and a touch of bright color here and there for contrast. If the bright colors are used sparingly as jewels, they give the pleasing effect of being precious. The House of God should not appear as a monotonous place; people are to be invited in — not driven out. Cool greens, blues, or grays may be used to create a restful atmosphere, but they should be relieved by splashes of the warm colors — red and yellow.

In recent years new color combinations have been used which are not based upon the primary colors. The method or explanation does not matter if the result is accepted by all as a pleasing effect. Black and white are combined to please the eye and black is combined with various colors. The device is not new, since black was used by the ancient Egyptians and Greeks. But new color combinations have come into favor and the pastor who is planning to have his church decorated would do well to locate a pleasing color combination found elsewhere.

Light and Shade

The most annoying error of church decoration is improper shading. Even when good colors are used, there is often too great a contrast in heaviness and a lack of proportion. The wrong lines and masses are emphasized. This fault may be observed even in a photograph or news print. In the pictures of many church interiors one sees at first glance a white altar, above which several triangles and a group of cherubs seem to dangle in mid-air. On second glance only is the church seen to have walls, pillars, and a vaulted ceiling.

The remedy is simple. Give everything its proper prominence. The altar is the center of prominence, but it should harmonize in design, color, and emphasis with the rest of the interior. It should appear to be a part of the church. The lines of architecture may be slightly emphasized, but most prominence should be given to walls and pillars, as they must not only support the roof but must actually appear to be doing so. An almost universal fault is to have a ceiling painted in heavy colors or timbered in dark wood and the side walls painted in a light tint. Such an interior is oppressive. The ceiling gives the impression of being about to fall at any moment. Beneath it, there can be no material aid to any elevation of soul. The remedy here is to paint the ceiling in colors lighter than those of the side walls or else to make the side walls heavier with pictures and ornament.

Unpainted walls of old monastery chapels acquire the appearance of strength with age by a deepening of color and shadows. An irregular wall, broken by niches and transepts which show the thickness of the walls, has the appearance of strength. Where timbered ceilings are used, a visible support may be shown by *corbels* projecting from the wall, or by *pendent posts* extending part way down the side walls, or by *pendentive bracketing* or *hammer beams* reaching out from the wall to support the ceiling trusses. Exposed ceiling trusses are an advance in logical construction but they should not attract too much attention. The walls are more important.

The beauty of Gothic stone vaults was in the appearance of lightness attained in the use of heavy stone. Timbered ceilings were used in Gothic churches, mostly in England, as a temporary arrangement, with the intention of replacing them later with stone vaulting. Many of them have a rugged simplicity. They are not the best form of Gothic but they produce a homelike effect conducive to devotion. Polychrome effects are usually better than a mass of dark timber; the colors have a brighter, more cheerful effect.

Historic Decoration

Wall painting need not be done in a strictly historical manner. It should be modified according to local conditions and present taste. It has two purposes — to please God as a thank offering by showing respect for His earthly dwelling place, and to aid the devotion of those who come thither to pray. The offering of civilized people to God should not be crude and primitive, but should be the best that can be given. If the church were only a votive offering, the taste of the people might be ignored. But it is a structure built for worship. The very building is a sacramental — "something blessed by the Church to excite devotion." So the final effect must be pleasing to the people who make use of the church. People may sometimes praise work done in bad taste because of the unusualness of it, but tasteless novelty soon becomes tiresome and annoying. Decoration done in good taste rarely fails to please.

There is no reason, historical, artistic, or liturgical, for decorating churches during the twentieth century in the same manner as during the sixth. There would be some reason for so decorating a basilica, newly erected in the city of Rome, because it might be expected to be similar to other basilicas. But elsewhere the Basilican plan of structure would be a sufficient reminder of the past and the wall decoration should suit the preferences of living people. Old colors may be used, but the figures should be modern. The most appropriate style would be that found in the catacombs, although it is rarely used at present. We sometimes see American churches decorated in the Byzantine style, but that was a foreign style in ancient Rome and is doubly so in America. In Rome it is a reminder of decline and Oriental domination. Had Rome retained independence and culture, there would have been a group of native artists to decorate churches in a Roman

[147]

style. We of the present have no political reason for using the style of another section of the globe, especially when that style is ancient. We do not need it as a reminder of the antiquity of the Church, for this is familiar to everyone. Besides, the religious symbols and ceremonies are further reminders of it.

The dark color combinations of the Orient are beautiful but we wish our interiors, and especially the ceilings, to be light. Heavy, all-over decorations are not used in other instances at present and should not be used in churches. Marble incrustation and mosaic cannot be imitated in painting. It is a fundamental law of art that each medium must keep within its own limitations. The natural colors of stone and marble harmonize better than a mixture of artificial pigments. Mosaic is the most beautiful and lasting of all wall decoration. Its imitation is only an imitation. In most parishes not more than a dozen members have been in Rome and, therefore, the historical significance of Byzantine ornament is lost. The great amount of time and money expended on such decoration is wasted.

Romanesque Decoration

The Romanesque style was developed in the beginning of a new Christian culture before the art of painting was rediscovered. Historically, then, it makes no demand for painted walls. It was developed by the Benedictine monks and calls for a hint of monastic severity. It was a rugged style, with stone carving as its principal ornament.

Most of the American round-arch churches of the past generation were inspired by the Romanesque Revival of Richardson, but their interiors show no understanding of the style. They were decorated in the Renaissance style, which is extreme in its refinement and is the very opposite of feudal austerity. A Romanesque church should have stone or brick interior walls, with just enough color in the sanctuary for contrast. If the walls are of lime plaster,

INTERIOR, ST. FLORIAN'S CHURCH, DETROIT, MICH.

Cram and Ferguson, Architects, Boston, Mass. Decoration by Conrad Schmitt Studios

Architectural lines are allowed their proper importance. Plain wall mass in a neutral color is relieved by high lights of bright colors. Harmony of color in walls, altar, and windows.

they could be painted in a solid color to give the effect of monastic simplicity.

The Lombard style, now being revived, had more refinement than contemporary styles in other countries, as classical tradition had been preserved in Italy. But the Lombard style, also, emerged from the age of darkness and should be kept rather plain, although it now admits of more ornament than was employed in the original churches of that style.

Gothic Decoration

Here in America we have scarcely acquired the Gothic spirit. We have many churches with pointed-arch windows and pointed spires, but very few good Gothic churches. Gothic allows rich decoration, but there must be a background of massive outline, since it is a stone-construction style. On this general rule we must insist, for Gothic is a style of logical structure. The architectural outlines must be preserved and the painted ornament must be so shaded as to be of secondary importance. If bands must be painted across the ceiling to represent ribbed vaulting, the vaults should have more emphasis in color and shading than the lines which divide them. This is another way of saying that the wall is more important than the painted decorations upon it.

Ruskin and his non-Catholic followers preferred plain walls, since they found them so in old churches. But originally they were not so. Time and the Reformation destroyed many of the wall paintings of the Gothic age. Viollet-le-Duc found traces of considerable colored ornament in old churches. Catholic tradition is in favor of color, as our churches must be cheerful. We wish to enjoy a visit to our Father's house. Some of the Gothic churches built a few years ago, with interiors of stone or brick and no color anywhere except in windows, were too gloomy to be devotional. But now the mauve period belongs to the past.

Like the Romanesque style, however, Gothic too is monastic in origin and should be restrained in ornament. The great cathedrals, in which master artists spent their lifework, and carved and painted with divinely guided hands, show the virtue of temperance. The rich ornament is restrained within structural lines and the colors are shaded into submission. If we could find an artist, now, thoroughly conversant with Catholic discipline, we might allow him to be lavish with his brush, but a painter who regards his work as of greater importance than that of the architect is excluded by the law of logic.

Renaissance Ornament

A great many of our church decorators came from the land in which the Renaissance flourished. People of that race are artistic by nature and tradition, but they have seen so much bad art mixed with the good that their taste is confused. If not directed they would be instinctively inclined to paint a church interior in the Baroque style, as that is the last church style which flourished in Italy. It has its merits and it was once fashionable, but that was long ago. In the height of popularity an illogical style may be tolerated, but when it has gone out of fashion it is out forever. Italian artists are good draftsmen and careful in details, but their taste in color differs from the American taste.

By a strange reversal Americans now lead the world in color harmony and in delicacy of choice, while a few years ago they knew nothing about such things and were not even interested. Now almost every home shows some evidence of a love for color and refinement of taste. But Italian artists of the present day are inclined toward bright hues and harsh combinations. They give equal value to all colors and no one color predominates. All are spread on the wall and allowed to fight for supremacy. If Italian artists could be directed to work in American color combinations, the result would be inspiring by its beauty.

Many decorators come from Germany and their selection of color combinations is equally bad. The German Baroque was less pleasing than the Italian, and church decorators seem to lag behind present developments in decoration. The German interpretation of the "New Art" movement was not pleasing, even when popular, and it is now out of date and not used anywhere except in churches. There was reason for a modernistic movement in Germany as a protest against the past.

We do not wish to shut out any nationality from work in American churches. We propose only that they fall in line with local tradition and taste. There are no art schools to direct them in church decoration, but a short course at any art school would teach them color harmony which could be applied to traditional church symbolism by their own ingenuity.

The early Renaissance was really classical, and a modern church of that style should be decorated in the classical spirit. The late Renaissance was a riotous revolution against all traditional form and color. It is appropriate for a million-dollar theater, where the eyes are to be dazzled for a few minutes between the acts, but it is the very opposite to the spirit of prayer. If the architect has planned a church in the Renaissance style, the decorator should use his brush with reserve in an attempt to create a dignified, restful interior. The atmosphere of the theater and of the church are directly opposite. If theatrical music is objectionable, theatrical decoration is more inappropriate as being more obvious.

One of the faults of this style of decoration is the drawing of angels as pagan cherubs, or cupids. The ancient pagans represented the soul as the genius of a person. The genii were represented as cupids. In the early Renaissance Fra Angelico represented angels with wings and flowing garments. Later, as interest in paganism increased, angels were represented as pagan genii. Today, if we use the Renaissance style, there is no need of preserving pagan symbolism. Undraped cupids are intruders and should be excluded. The angels of Fra Angelico are better Christians.

If stencils are used in church decoration, there should be some variety of color or form introduced by free-hand. If an ornamental band is seen to be exact the eye does not follow it, as it is known to be the same all around the church. But if there is variety, interest is created. Standardization is more objectionable in art than anywhere else. The eyes soon tire of machine-made monotony.

Walls are not something of which to be ashamed. It used to be the custom to cover every square foot of space with an all-over pattern. But ceilings cannot be held up by grapevines and especially painted ones. Walls are presumed to be present, but they should be in evidence. A tinted wall with no other decoration gives the idea of strength and architectural purpose. If painted ornament can add anything to that impression, it is worth while. If not, its omission would be a gain.

The Church can do a service to art by reviving the custom of having paintings as altar screens. Being in colors, they are more pleasing to the eye than statues of cold marble, although statues also have their purpose. If there were a demand, great artists would be found. Many famous paintings in Europe were done as altarpieces and many old churches attract visitors from afar to see an inspired altar panel. That sort of adornment would create a new interest in American churches.

Interior Harmony

The most important artistic quality in a church interior is harmony. It is a unity attained by the good design of the architect, understood and followed by the decorator, and completed by well-designed altars and church furniture. If there be harmony in the final result, colors will blend properly, the altar will be prominent but not too conspicuous, and every line and form will add to the general pleasing effect. But such harmony is not easily attained and has been rare in years past. There is almost always overemphasis of some features. There may be a beautiful marble altar in a dark, drab church. Or the windows may stand out and draw attention away from the walls and altar. Or the mural decoration may be harsh in color and contradictory in line, weakening the appearance of the walls. Wooden altars and Communion rails may be white and everything else dark.

The remedy lies in the cultivation of better taste and in knowledge of the rules of artistic harmony. The furnishing cannot be left entirely to an architect, as he must finally leave the building to the pastor, and the whole effect can be spoiled by so small an item as an altar cloth of pointed lace breaking up the horizontal lines of the altar. Urging the leaving of the entire plan to one man is like insisting on everyone voting without telling them how to vote. They might vote for the wrong candidate. Not every architect is trustworthy and the same may be said in regard to decorators. *If the entire plan is to be intrusted to one man, he should be the best available.* When this slogan was first used there were scarcely any architects able to produce a praiseworthy plan. Now a great many can do so, but not all.

Even in new developments there is danger of standardization. A new church is praised for the beauty of its design and immediately several similar churches are erected elsewhere. This custom is not entirely blameworthy, as it leads to a general improvement in taste and to better construction, but there would be more artistic perfection if each design were somewhat different from the others. An improvement should be made on the original.

Interior decorators could aid greatly in attaining interior harmony, but many of them are unreliable. Instead of trusting the work to them it is necessary for the pastor to be on his guard lest they destroy the beauty and harmony of the interior.

The only way out, then, is for the pastor to take an interest in better churches and develop his taste, which will be shown in the church over which he presides. He should know something about the style of architecture used and the kind of decoration it requires. He should know something about color harmony and proportion. Members of the parish would be helpful in the selection of a proposed sketch for decoration. It is unreasonable to insist that people of the parish should approve of new decoration merely because it was expensive. If, in fact, the decoration is archaic and inharmonious in color, no amount of talking will make it pleasing to parishioners.

One reason for the lack of harmony in American churches is the buying of furnishings from various sources. Altars are imported from Italy and windows from Germany, without consultation with the American architect. Each country has a national taste which should be considered. Darkly painted windows, with heavy landscape and complicated architectural lines, do not fit in with the simplicity of present design of American churches. We do not criticize the source of the windows, but there is need of new designs, simple in outline, with less detail, and with no painted architecture. The windows may be made in Germany, but they should be designed in America.

Stained-Glass Windows

Our windows are too large. Stained-glass windows were developed for the medieval Gothic cathedrals which used buttresses for walls and filled in the intervening space with glass. The object was to create a spirit of delicacy. Now we strive for the very opposite effect — strength. Our modern Gothic churches are not daintily balanced and do not juggle stone vaulting high in the air. We prefer the heavy walls of English Gothic. We must take one style or the other. A massive wall requires small deep-set windows. In the ancient cathedrals the variety of outline prevented all windows being seen from one location, but in our pillarless naves, with unbroken wall lines, every window is seen at once. The sight of a group of windows does not give the idea of strength and, without the high vaulted ceiling, we fail to express either strength or delicacy.

In many churches a reduced size of window would be an improvement, as it is possible to have too much rich color. But we cannot get along without colored windows. Although they were not used before the Gothic age, they are now required for all churches. A new church in which the windows have not been installed is never striking in beauty, and it lacks the atmosphere of devotion which colored light alone can give.

Windows are intended to give light and color rather than for a pictorial purpose. Glass is a different medium from painting and should be handled in a different way. Perspective and scenery cannot be shown in a window, since it is to be treated as a flat surface. Many imported windows are covered with opaque paint allowing the light to show through in some few places. If we wish paintings, the wall is the place for them. Windows are intended for light.

One of America's great artists, John LaFarge, besides putting mural painting on a high level, improved the art of stained glass. Although a painter, he considered windows a medium for color rather than for pictured landscape. He spent long hours seeking new colors. He shaded glass by superimposing an extra thickness and rejoiced over a new shade as over the finding of a jewel. The American development of jeweled windows is largely due to his research in colors and materials, fifty years ago. The best window glass is now made in America, and since windows are not to be treated as paintings the most brilliant color effects are obtained in American glass.

There is an old dispute as to whether painted pictures should be decorative or should exist for themselves, independent of architecture. A picture or window by LaFarge would be worthy of independence. A church favored with one of these would be interesting and would inspire devotion. But lesser artists should consider the general ensemble and make the window or painting a part of the whole design in line and color. A picture or window above the main altar might well be striking in character, as it would help to attract attention to the altar. But side windows and paintings on side walls should be part of the general design.

It is difficult to overestimate the influence of beautiful, devo-

Within the image: IOACHIM·AND·ANN·OFFERING TO·THE·LORD·THEIR·CHILD THE·EVER·BLESSED·MARY

PICTURE OF THE PRESENTATION, ST. ANSELM'S CHURCH,
NEW YORK, N. Y.
Picture of the Presentation of Mary in the Temple. An example of the stately
dignity of Beuronese decoration. It is decorative rather than realistic.

[157]

ALTAR VESSELS, ST. ANSELM'S CHURCH, NEW YORK, N. Y.
Specially designed for the church by Benedictine artists, in the Beuronese Style.

tional, and well-adapted stained-glass windows, picturing first in delicately chosen tints and living colors the life of our Divine Lord, of His Blessed Mother, and of the saints. Like the statues and paintings, when unified into one great and dignified design embracing the entire church, these pictures are lasting sermons giving instruction and inspiration to the congregation and to everyone who sees them. But all should and can be done in harmony with the general light, color, and architectural effect, to create the atmosphere of worship, where nothing disturbs and all lifts up the soul to God.

The harmonizing of mural decoration with architecture was emphasized by the convert artist Overbeck, leader of the Nazarites, who did so much for church art in the middle of the nineteenth century. Born in Germany, he studied the works of the old masters in Rome, and as leader of a new school he taught the decorative as well as pictorial value of painting. His paintings have an architectural value in color and design. By insisting on harmony between painting and architecture he started a new school of painting and mural art which continued long after his death.

Beuronese Style

Artists of Beuron Abbey in Germany, no doubt, were influenced by the theories of Overbeck. Father Desiderius and two companions designed and decorated the St. Maurus Chapel in 1869–71, and later joined the Benedictine Order. The chapel is the cradle of the Beuron or Benedictine style. A brief reference is made to the style in *Yesterdays of an Artist-Monk*, published by Kenedy and Sons. Father Desiderius is quoted as finding his inspiration in early Christian and Byzantine artists, in Giotto, and in the rhythm of Egyptian and Greek temples. He found in the ancients a mathematical proportion which he adopted. "It was my dream," he says, "to elevate all modern art, and to lead it back, purified and perfected by measurement, from a state of individual weakness to one of classical beauty."

[159]

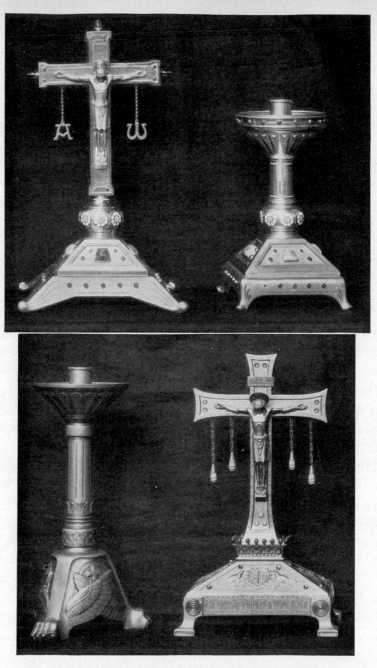

ALTAR FURNISHINGS, ST. ANSELM'S CHURCH,
NEW YORK, N. Y.

Specially designed for their purpose. The Beuronese style of
art is sufficiently flexible to be suited to any kind of church.

If Father Desiderius had made an original design for the structure of the chapel, he would have made a still greater contribution to church art. As it is, his style is only for decoration. He designed the chapel in the manner of a Greek temple. In opposition to the theory which we have already expressed, that the people should be pleased by the design, we read that Father Desiderius met considerable opposition. His work was considered new and strange and was not popular. But that was long ago.

Twenty years ago the crypt of Monte Cassino Abbey, in Italy, was beautifully decorated by a Benedictine artist trained at Beuron. It is surprising what an artist can make of a square room without architectural lines. Soft browns were used and black and white. Perpendicular geometric lines give a measured stateliness. Pictures of saints have a penetrating, spiritual expression, something of which may be found in certain Egyptian statues. An ancient Egyptian statue of basalt, with hands resting on knees, has no naturalistic likeness to the human form, but the eyes seem to search one's soul. Lifeless stone seems to have been endowed with eternal wisdom. Greek sculptors approached nearer to nature but missed spirituality. The Beuron artists turned to higher purposes whatever they could learn from the study of contemplative spirituality as this might be found in Egyptian art.

In the Beuron style the garments of saints and monks hang straight without folds, which gives the formal effect of Byzantine art, although the faces are natural and modern. The straight lines make the style well suited to mural art. Curved lines would break architectural lines, but straight lines harmonize with the architecture. A quotation from Ruskin will best explain the effect.

"All the noble draperies, either in painting or sculpture (color and texture being at present out of our consideration) have, so far as they are anything more than necessities, one of two great functions; they are the exponents of motion and gravitation. They are the most valuable means of expressing past as well as present motion in the figure, and they are almost the only means of indicating to the eye the force of gravity which resists such

[161]

motion. The Greeks used drapery in sculpture for the most part as an ugly necessity, but availed themselves of it gladly in all representation of action, exaggerating the arrangements of it which express lightness in the material, and follow gesture in the person. The Christian sculptors, caring little for the body, or disliking it, and depending exclusively on the countenance, received drapery at first contentedly as a veil, but soon perceived a capacity of expression in it which the Greek had not seen or had despised. The principal element of this expression was the entire removal of agitation from what was so preëminently capable of being agitated. It fell from their human forms plumb down, sweeping the ground heavily, and concealing the feet, while the Greek drapery was often blown away from the thigh. The thick and coarse stuffs of the monkish dresses, so absolutely opposed to the thin and gauzy web of antique material, suggested simplicity of division as well as weight of fall. There was no crushing or dividing them. And thus the drapery gradually came to represent the spirit of repose as it before had of motion, repose saintly and severe. The wind had no power upon the garment, as the passion none upon the soul" (Chapter, "The Lamp of Beauty").

The Beuron style uses geometric motifs borrowed from the Egyptians. An improvement would be the use of motifs from nature in the same mathematical rhythm. Although it is a logical and beautiful style when used by artists of great ability, we hesitate to recommend the style for general use, as it would lead to extreme mannerisms or formalism. In fact, independent effort is better than adherence to any style. But from this consideration of an excellent form of decoration we may learn how to improve all church decoration. St. Anselm's Church, in New York, was decorated in the Beuron style by Fra Adelbert, of Monte Cassino. The work of such an artist must be a good example.

We have criticized the present use of Byzantine decorations. It could be as excellent as the Beuron style if painted imitation of mosaic were avoided, and if the design were less crowded and the colors more subdued and harmonious. There is an effect of marvelous power in a picture in which the body is in absolute repose but the face is blazing with animation.

One of the marks of the best modern building planning and ornamentation is the unconscious use of an ancient classical rule. The Greeks built with ornate simplicity. Their ruined temples have a dignity rarely attained since their time even by Greek revivals, which usually ran to excess. But, strange to say, the present age which works and plays in rapid syncopated time erects buildings in classical rhythm. The secret is in the proper balance of structural mass and ornament. Unadorned concrete piers are contrasted by rich ornament in a doorway or window. The classical rule was called the two-to-three rule; two parts decoration to three parts plain wall mass. That rule is now commonly used in exterior and interior design. Before this age of better taste every foot of space, exterior or interior, was covered with ornament. Now we are more thoughtful of contrast and background. We know that ornament is more effective if used sparingly. For a while after the awakening we left our church interiors dull and cold as a protest against excess of ornament. The next step was the sparing use of rich colors on a background of plain wall mass. In fifteen years we have gone farther in good church design than in the previous four centuries.

Present design is good, but the execution is too mechanically perfect. Modern efficiency is everywhere in evidence. There is rapidity of construction with the completion bargained for to take place at a very definite and not very distant period. There is, further, the strength of concrete to support any desired weight. There is the brightness, too, of polished metal. Ornament, though seemingly carved, has been molded and stamped by factory machines. All is straight and correct with no waste of space or material. Exteriors are smart and new, but that is not art. Churches erected in that manner and spirit will keep off the rain, but they are not suited to prayer.

Chapter XI

MODERN ARCHITECTURE

THE admirable attempts of original design in commercial buildings recently erected in America are based on the slogan "Living
Architecture," which was used first by Ruskin, who was always
sound in theory even if he sometimes acted on prejudice in its
application. In his chapter entitled "The Lamp of Life," in the
Seven Lamps of Architecture, that great critic gives originality
as the foundation of good architecture. He approves of borrowing from the past, as even the greatest artists have done, but
the borrower must add something from his own imagination.
Music uses sound and painting uses color, both gifts of nature,
but a builder uses for his wall dead stone, which has no beauty
but only strength. If the stone is to be given beauty it must be
added to other stones and a building erected with balance and
proportion which shows the rational plan of the builder and not
a mere haphazard heaping of stones. Finally, as a greater proof
of intelligent planning, there must be some carving on the stone
to represent ideas which the stone itself could never convey. The
continuous improvement in the plans of former nations, the
adaptation of them to present conditions, and the addition of
carving that truly represents the genius of the present age, constitute, according to Ruskin, a "living art."

Some of the appeal which a definite manner of building and
ornamentation possess comes from tradition, the memory of great
artists who have added their contributions to the style. In this
sense, surely, it is allowable to respect the past. It is not expected
that each generation will start anew from nothing, but as Ruskin
writes: "Now, in the first place — and this is rather an important
point — it is no sign of deadness in a present art that it borrows
or imitates, but only if it borrows without paying interest, or if
it imitates without choice."

[164]

That is exactly what America and all the world has done. Until recently all nations have "borrowed without paying interest" and imitated without any sign of intelligence. Churches of the thirteenth century were copied in the nineteenth, without adaptation to the time. Copies of a steeple from one church and windows, doors, and altars from others were all thrown together, without thought to the fact that the parts did not match. It was worse than the custom of Rome in her decline, of taking marble pillars from ruined temples and using them for Christian churches. They were of all colors and sizes, and such as were particularly short had to be pieced out to serve their purpose. And while some justification could be found for all this in that it saved expense and labor, nevertheless, the period which that spirit represented is called the Dark Age.

Some time later, aspiring people, in search of the light, imitated crudely the Roman ruins about them. But they proceeded further and dared to improve the structure of vaulted roofs in the Romanesque style. The beginning of that inventive effort goes back to what are called the Dark Ages. What, then, of an age in which there was no originality and yet when men at the same time prided themselves on their supposedly great accomplishments.

Until a few years ago Catholic churches were as uninspiring as they could well have been made. The same was true of other churches, and of public and domestic buildings everywhere, but we are interested now in churches only. These edifices frequently were pretentious, yet vulgar, copies of great churches of the past. Interiors were dull and gloomy. Not in four centuries had anyone introduced an original idea in either structure or decoration. The great upheaval of the sixteenth century and the struggle for existence which followed it seemed to have deadened all initiative. Architecturally, the Church lived in the past.

In her early history the Church had gone through several long and dismal centuries, trying to forget the ancient paganism. But with the pagan Renaissance the ugly monster was brought back to life by misguided Christians and ever since that time the world has been disgusted with art. But what we here mean by art is not luxurious refinement. It is the erection of houses of worship which will give to God the honor due Him from His creatures and which will not bring discredit on the Church.

Because of sins committed in its name, the word *art* carries with it in our day a suggestion of affectation. We do not like the word, but we cannot substitute a better one. When we use it here we mean true church art, the honest construction of churches and the beautifying of them as an act of worship. The builders of Gothic churches did not think of themselves as architects and artists. They were classified thus by later generations. Their one purpose was to honor and glorify God, and if in doing so they followed rules and formed themselves into organizations, that was only incidental. By church art, then, we mean an act of devotion.

Because it was the Church that had always taken the leadership in art, it followed that when she relinquished her interest there was no other guide, for secular art had also lost its inspiration. For those familiar with the art galleries of Europe, this requires no more than the mere statement. Sacred Art came to an end in the sixteenth century. Since that period, in Europe as well as in America, all buildings have been copied from the past without applying any originality.

In Europe there was a historical reason for the use of old styles, but in the United States no such tradition had been handed down. A new use of Greek and Roman styles in Europe could be called a revival, but not so in the United States, since that which did not previously exist could not be revived. Yet we find Greek and Roman temples and basilicas erected here as public buildings. If in the distant future, the historical records of this country should be lost, scholars searching the ruins of the past might come to the conclusion that America was once a Roman province, because its national and state capitols and other public buildings were designed by long-dead architects of the ancient Roman Empire.

From time to time, there have been, in Europe and America, stirrings of the artistic soul, but the result has never been more than the revival of an ancient style. The Pugins renewed interest in the Gothic style in England, while, in quite recent times, there has been a Gothic revival, or beginning, in America. The Catholic architects — Bentley in England, Cuypers in Holland, and Comes in America — showed originality in handling old styles, but they died with their work unfinished. Due to the new coöperative movement, living architects are now showing a general improvement. Buildings erected since the World War are really meritorious.

There was some reason, as we have just implied, why the builders of England and Continental Europe might be interested in ancient styles but there was no such justification in America. Our builders seem to have labored under what in the cant phrase of our day is called an "inferiority complex." Our secular architecture consisted of Greek and Roman temples, Renaissance buildings from all nations, and even Oriental mosques and Chinese pagodas. In some of our cozy summer resorts, hidden away in the mountains, we still find, instead of American lodges, Swiss "chalets." There has always been a lack of respect for anything native. The very opposite is the logical point of view.

Native Art Only is Genuine

In this age which boasts of progress, great initiative, and unprecedented wealth, there was, until recently, no progress in building. A great deal of money and effort was spent on buildings, but everything produced was a mediocre copy. Even a perfect copy would have been second-rate work, but our own copies were not even well done. Ornamental detail was copied without understanding of structural principles. Sometimes the styles were mixed. We have seen Gothic altars in Renaissance churches and, almost always, the various structures of a parish group have been of as many different styles as there were buildings.

Our progress was long retarded by art schools, with their absolute rules drawn from measurement of famous old buildings. They ignored Christianity and were interested only in the classic works of ancient paganism and the Renaissance version of them. There was a conspiracy of silence on the great Catholic art of medieval centuries. The improvement in church building, therefore, was due to independent effort, as it did not come from the schools. The lack of special instruction for church architects resulted in a series of poor copies of European churches. Peasant immigrants from Europe smiled at the cheapness of our architecture, which was unworthy of a country that took the lead in other things.

It should be considered a truism, but it may seem startlingly revolutionary to say, that architecture should be original. Originality is sought even by semicivilized makers of rugs and pottery, and yet for four centuries our church builders did not dare have an idea of their own. The ancient churches, it is true, set a high standard which may never be surpassed, but that does not prevent each age from having its own interpretation of traditional art.

Twelve years ago was started the publication of "The Catholic Art Bulletin" in the *Catholic Daily Tribune*. Appeals were made for a new interest in church building and decoration, and there was criticism of the general unworthiness of churches in our time. Since then there has been noted a gradual improvement and a more common interest in church art. Credit should be given to the "voice crying in the wilderness."

[168]

At the close of the year 1931 appeared the first number of the beautiful and finely illustrated *Liturgical Arts* quarterly, issued by the then newly formed Liturgical Arts Society. On that occasion *America* wrote: "All seem agreed that the most remarkable feature of the quarterly is the fact that it is not remarkable. Rather it is generally recognized as filling at last a recognized need" (December 12, 1931). That indeed was a great step forward.

Beginnings of Originality

Fifty years ago Richardson made popular an adaptation of the French Romanesque style. Richardson had an artistic sense of proportion and he would have planned noteworthy buildings in any style that he chose to use. Other architects employed the Romanesque style in a less artistic way and its use did not long survive the death of Richardson. As stated elsewhere, the exteriors of Catholic churches in the Romanesque style were well designed, but the interiors did not continue the style. The same was true of the use of Gothic both before and after the Civil War. The exteriors of our churches were good, but the interiors showed no understanding of the style. Interiors cannot be copied from photographs so easily as exteriors. Each one requires special treatment. The early Gothic and Romanesque exteriors were not remarkable works of art, but they were passable attempts at erecting worthy churches in a land which was not blessed with the presence of great ancient churches. But the interiors were illogically constructed and horribly painted, while the people were satisfied with ugliness. Had there been any demand for improvement of churches the Romanesque style would have been a good starting point, since it was not like the old Romanesque churches, but was an original adaptation of the style. A demand for better artists would have brought them forth, but there was no demand and the artists did not appear.

A little later another chance for originality was missed when an original style used by Louis Sullivan for secular buildings was not adopted for churches. He decorated store fronts in his own florid manner not copied from the past. There was some little hint of the Romanesque in the heavy piers and low, round vaults and arches, but the flowery ornament was unlike anything classical or Gothic. It received but little praise and was not imitated, but now it is recognized as an inventive contribution to American architecture. Because he did not follow the crowd, Sullivan was bitterly criticized and died in poverty and despair.

Sullivan designed the Transportation Building for the Chicago World's Fair of 1893. It was brilliant with color and ornament and a contrast to the other buildings which were of classic design. As a result of the Fair the classic styles prevailed for a long period following. The "New Art" movement, which started a few years later in France, was somewhat similar to the Sullivan style and may have been inspired by it. This statement, we are aware, has never previously been made by writers on art and cannot be substantiated now by any claim to special research.

The "New Art" was utilized mainly for ornament. It was adopted in the manufacture of church windows imported from Europe, especially in those with geometric designs. While rarely recognized here as "New Art," the style nevertheless had an influence on all decoration of the time. It was used in this country in painted ornamentation of interiors by artists who came from France and Germany. Italian decorators have always been loyal to the Renaissance and Baroque.

Modern Painting

Modern painting and modern architecture are based on different theories and have no relation to each other. We must introduce here a brief discussion of modern painting — just long enough to reject the entire movement.

All great painters manifested originality of some kind. Some invented new color combinations; others had recourse to simplicity of design; still others elaborated scenic backgrounds. Before photography was invented, there may have been a few paintings of historical subjects made for no other purpose than to preserve the scene in its objective reality. But usually there was question of an interpretation.

In a portrait, predominant virtues were represented by the expression of countenance, even by slight exaggeration. Michelangelo represented greatness of character by gigantic size. Similar devices were employed by others. No artist was expected to imitate nature slavishly. The same is true even of photography. The photographer tries to catch an expression of genial good humor, which may not be the normal expression, yet mirrors the subject's better self. An effect of light and shade gives an idealized appearance, somewhat as the halo about the head of a saint. Throughout the history of painting there has been rivalry between the idealists and the realists. When one group drifted too far away from nature, another group insisted on a return to it. The modernistic painters are all idealists even when they call themselves realists. There are many groups, but all paint, not what they see but what is in their own minds.

The artist Paul Ninas was quoted by Eleanor Early in a recent article as saying: "Our creed is to exaggerate. We love extravagance. We stiffen the symmetry of our trees. We stress to the point of deformation the curves of a lovely woman. We make our roses too red, and our lilies too white. Our grass is too green, and our oceans too blue. We want our canvases to be exhilarating, ecstatic, and profoundly vital."

Our comment on that statement is that a slight exaggeration would convey the idea intended, but when nature is completely ignored and there is no connection between the object and its supposed representation the canvas may easily be "exhilarating" and "ecstatic," but certainly it is not "vital."

[171]

In one of a recent series of articles on modern art, published in the *Corriere D'America,* Mario Girardon says that modern artists go beneath the outward appearance of an object to find "the internal fire of things." They are "children who break toys to see how they are made." A man has hands, arms, a head, etc., and a machine has wheels. The more important parts are represented and for the moderns that is enough. "The generic inspiration of the work, which is that which most attracts the profane, is that which is of least importance to the contemporaneous artists." And a little later: "Hence the essential fact that the object, of itself, has no importance, but there is supreme importance in the manner in which it is represented." In other words, neither the object represented nor those who see the picture are of any importance. Only the artist is important. That point of view must exclude modern art from Catholic churches. In the church the object represented comes first, being Christ or the saints. Those who see the paintings come next, as church paintings must aid devotion. The artist must have sufficient humility to place himself last. Elsewhere we have already seen how the improvement of painting and the other decorative arts brought about the decline of church architecture, when the church became for the artist merely four walls over which to spread out his ornament. Such was not the spirit of Fra Angelico. He was not a great artist from the point of view of technique, as his lines were often crudely drawn, but he was great in religious art, for his pictures breathed the spirit of reverence.

Not merely from the point of view of religious art, but from any point of view, modern painting must be condemned. It is subjective rather than objective. It pretends to represent something and does not do so. Its interpretation of the object is so completely divorced from the object itself that no meaning is conveyed to the beholder. Painters may find some interest in studying the imaginative work of others, but their interest relates to ideas and not to objective reality. It concerns psychology and not art. It is like crystal gazing, where one looks at a glass ball and allows the mind to wander to thoughts of Alpine palaces and idle pleasure. The dreams may be pleasant enough, but they have no objective reality and we have no time to listen to the narration of them.

The one benefit we have received from the various modern extremists is the love for color. The appreciation of color harmony was very rare until recently. Dead grays were the favorite colors. But now, thanks to the modernists, there is color everywhere and life has been made happier by it.

Modern Architecture

Painting and architecture are two different arts. Usually they go together, but then painting must be subservient. When Renaissance painters became great artists, architecture declined, since any sort of walls were satisfactory for mural painting.

There have been great churches without mural painting. Romanesque and Gothic churches used some colored ornament, but even after time had dimmed the color the churches still retained their beauty of form. It is quite possible, then, to reject outright all forms of painting which might be included in the term "modernistic," and still be interested in modern developments of architecture. They are two different movements.

Modernistic painting is revolutionary. It is a rebellion against tradition, beauty, form, proportion, light and shade, facts of nature, and, strange to say, even against the paint brush itself, since the paint is often applied directly from the tube without the aid of a brush. In that case it is not painting at all; it is a plastic art. It has produced some interesting things, because anything new is interesting, but it is not a pictorial art, because it does not represent nature. It can represent thought in a better way than the old method of picturing a scene in a cloud above the dreamer's head, but the interpretation is not obvious. The beholder is left to imagine what he pleases. Modernistic painting, then, is a rebellion against reality.

But modernistic architecture cares for reality alone. It builds for utility and ignores not merely ornament but all beauty of form. It is intensely practical, which means that it is intensely selfish, as there is no consideration for what the neighbors think of it. It lacks the community spirit and, therefore, is to be condemned as lacking in one of the important purposes of architectural design, which is to lend added attractiveness to the pleasing appearance of the city. It is not as illogical as modernistic painting, since it does not deny reality, but it rejects beauty and, so in turn, we must reject that sort of architecture, as it fails to fulfill its purpose.

But in doing so we have no intention to reject originality and inventiveness. It is unfortunate that at the very time when America seemed to be preparing for a worth-while contribution to the art of church building, there should spring up other movements to confuse the issue. Not everything new is modernistic, and an appeal for improvement is not, necessarily, a rebellion against the past. There is also a modern architecture which is praiseworthy but we are not constrained to follow it. We are concerned first of all with the needs of the Church, and there was a demand for better church architecture before the appearance of modern secular architecture.

At the risk of repetition we must insist on the need for creative architecture. Conservatives would have us cling to the old, but that would mean the death of art itself, since in the days of real art the Church was never for a single moment satisfied with things as they were. There was continual aspiration for better things — finite man trying to attain the infinite. When we deal with fundamental principles there is always opposition to change, but in practical applications it is not so, since everyone enjoys that which is new as well as beautiful.

CHARITY CRUCIFIXION TOWER, LITTLE FLOWER SHRINE,
ROYAL OAK, MICH.

Henry J. McGill, Architect, New York, N. Y.

Showing the strength of stone. An original but conservative modern
method of design.

CHURCH ARCHITECTURE

The traveler in Europe soon learns to look for originality. If the cathedrals of Rheims, Chartres, and Paris were all the same except for length and height, there would be no need of going to see each one. The sight of one would include them all. But the interest in small churches as well as cathedrals is due to the knowledge that each is different from the rest. So the traveler examines the altars, the windows, the carving of pews and choir stalls, and every bit of painting on the walls, knowing that in this place the townsmen made an original contribution to the art of Christendom, and that nowhere else in all the world will he be able to see what he sees here. A single door or a window may be an inventive work of art to be remembered throughout a lifetime.

The same should be true in America, but it is not so. The traveler in a strange city, motoring past, may, without stopping, see that a church is standardized Gothic or Romanesque, and he knows at once, without any inspection, what the interior is like. It is the same as hundreds of other churches he has seen in various parts of the country. If there are pictures on the walls, they will be copies of old masters. There is nothing new, nothing that required thought, and hence nothing within that is artistic. The building might almost as well have consisted merely of four straight walls. Money spent on plagiaristic ornament is money wasted. How much more inviting the church would be to the passer-by if he could suspect the possibility of finding within an original bit of painting or an imaginative wood carving.

Modern facility of travel and communication are largely to blame. Each section of the country knows what is being constructed in every other section and finds it easier to do the same than to think out something new. In medieval Europe travel was difficult and each community was left to itself. This led naturally to modifications in the styles of buildings seen elsewhere, or possibly only heard of and not even seen in pictures. Today nations have become closer neighbors, and the great works of architecture and painting of each country are well known to all the others. This should lead to improvements in art, but the modern desire for speed and easiness of effort has had the opposite effect. It has produced only copies.

Yet, strange to say, original design does not require great artistic ability. Small children in elementary schools are taught to represent a flower in conventional design and from a model to make half a dozen new designs inspired by it. Professional artists should be capable of doing the same if they are at all worthy of the name. Instead of repeating over and over a design which was beautiful in the original, they should be able, after studying its composition and effects of light and shade, to get the same effects in a new design.

Thus, for example, the classic acanthus leaf is represented in America, where it does not grow. The same effects could be attained by some other irregularly edged and curled leaf. The rich effect of an ancient Gothic entrance is due to elaborate carving, but we need not use the same motif. There are leaves and flowers which have never been seen in art. And if we prefer classic simplicity we need not build a duplicate of the Parthenon. We could study its excellent proportions and then, instead of round pillars, use square ones, grooved for variety if we so desired, and placed in double rows for depth, light, and shade, and we might carve a frieze that should present an American subject in an American style. The refined beauty of the Greek might be missing, but the effort would be much more admirable than a perfect copy of the Parthenon. The latter would be an admission of incompetence.

We may borrow from the past, if we "pay interest." We may learn from the great masters, yet, if we are to be worthy pupils, we must make an effort to add something of our own. Anyone can do that. An original work is not always excellent. But once we should have begun to be original the critics demand of us the necessary development, which could lead to beauty. But originality comes first.

PROPOSED SHRINE OF THE LITTLE FLOWER, ROYAL OAK, MICH.

Henry J. McGill, Architect, New York, N. Y.

A modern design churchlike in appearance. The cross-shaped ground plan is not new but the widening of the transepts toward the center of the church is an innovation giving a better view. The suppressed dome is in accord with contemporary building. The stepped arches of the windows are rectangular but suggestive of the Gothic spirit. The entire plan is a departure from tradition without loss of beauty and symbolism.

Let us not, however, imagine for all this that we can ignore the artistic accomplishments of the past. Despite opinions to the contrary, civilization did not begin yesterday. All the nations came "bringing gifts." Assyrians, Egyptians, Persians, Greeks, Romans, and the later peoples of the earth have come, adding something to tradition which we may take as a starting point of our work.

If in architecture one building was out of proportion, the next one became better. One nation tried a certain method of structure and it was found to be practical and pleasing to the eye. As a consequence, other nations in turn adopted it. Color came from the East, harmony, from the Greeks, and dignity, from the Romans.

Even if we invent new forms and new ornament, we must still employ them according to the rules of sound esthetics which have stood the test of ages. Modernistic painters take nothing from the past and, therefore, they fail. They might accomplish something if in using new color combinations and a new method of interpretation, they did not neglect to look at the same time to the past for rules of harmony, balance of composition, and beauty of line. Even the more radical of modern builders do not entirely ignore the past. They must use some structural methods which have been adopted before. And if the exteriors of our buildings are to have any beauty or to give any satisfaction, they must follow rules of proportion and rhythm which long ago were thought out by ancient builders.

Especially in Catholic art must we respect tradition. Every line of a church suggests memories of the past. A high nave with low side aisles means the end of martyrdom and the right to live. The round arch is a proof that a new civilization could emerge from darkness. The pointed arch is a reminder of the triumph of Christian civilization, and the dome recalls the greatest artists who ever lived. In building a modern church we cannot ignore the record written in lovingly carved spires, ascending as the smoke of incense, and in pictures and statues which seem to live and, in a manner, really speak to us.

All that is precious heritage. It cannot be equaled now — perhaps never. But no builder of Catholic churches wishes to forget the past. We may respect tradition and yet interpret the Church to our own age. We need not live entirely in the past. We need not claim that progress is impossible. If we cannot equal the great work of the past we need not feebly copy it. Our own weak efforts would be better, and if we do our best no more can be expected of us. Our connection with the past will be shown by pictures, altars, confessional, baptismal font, and by symbols of traditional use, even if treated in a new manner. It requires no great effort to be traditional; it is more difficult to be practical.

The Record of Originality

Although America is a comparatively young nation, examples of every historical style may be found here. Instead of doing as many other nations have done, starting out to build in a way which suited us, using the material at hand in the most natural way, we have copied the ideas of the Old World and very often the copy was not well done. One might imagine that a new colony would start at the beginning and by experience learn to build, but the colonists brought a knowledge of art with them.

The Colonial style was brought to us from Greece and Rome *via* England. By necessity it was adapted to pioneer conditions and thus has a native spirit. A few artists of ability came to the new land and their work is highly prized even now. Originality was shown in the design of church steeples and of domestic homes and furniture. Present interest in antique furniture is thus due to merit not equaled since.

Later the Greek revival found favor. It followed ancient plans too closely and, therefore, had less originality and less merit than the earlier Colonial style. The use of Gothic before and after the Civil War had the same faults as the Gothic revival in Europe. The style was not understood and structure was incorrect and

ST. JOSEPH'S CHURCH, SEATTLE, WASH.

A. H. Albertson, Architect, Seattle, Wash. Jos. W. Wilson and Paul Richardson, Associates

A concrete monolith. The plain unbroken wall mass shows the strength of concrete. The straight lines show the fluid quality of the material. Compactness represents unity of structure. The verticle tower is logical in design for the material used and the composition is churchlike in appearance.

[181]

illogical. There was originality but it was outweighed by serious faults. We have already discussed the American adaptation of Romanesque. When used by artists it had great merit, but usually, through lack of artistic ability, it was as common and dull as the red brick of which it was constructed. Sometimes, through lack of knowledge, it was mixed with Gothic, and Gothic steeples were built on Romanesque churches. In a similar manner the styles were mixed again in the interior. Everyone knew that something was wrong and a time of electicism set in. Famous churches of Europe, known to be constructed in good style, were simply copied. A small parish tried to imitate, with small effort and expense, a famous cathedral built by masters. An exact copy would have had some merit, but such attempted reproductions were feeble and unworthy efforts.

Then Cram, Goodhue, Ferguson, and others brought into prominence the use of Gothic, which had not entirely died out after the time of Renwick, the designer of St. Patrick's Cathedral, New York. These great architects employed the Gothic style with simplicity, majesty, and power. Their work is not so much an adaptation as a selection of the best in ancient Gothic. Not only have they erected many beautiful churches but Mr. Cram by his writing and lectures has been the leader of a campaign for better churches. The use of so excellent a style has improved American taste and created a demand for the union of beauty and worship.

The Flamboyant, or highly decorated Gothic style, has not been used in America. The massiveness of early Gothic is preferred, as being more suited to present conditions and taste. High steeples are no longer popular and ornament is used sparingly. But there is need of further modification. Gothic is the most logical and beautiful of all the ancient church styles, but it belongs to another age and cannot be transplanted without change to America. Its exclusive use would give apparent force to the

ENTRANCE DETAIL, ST. JOSEPH'S CHURCH, SEATTLE, WASH.

A. H. Albertson, Architect, Seattle, Wash. Jos. W. Wilson and Paul Richardson, Associates

Showing the use of concrete for molded ornament. The depth of the entrance suggests spiritual shelter.

groundless criticism that the Church is foreign to the American disposition and customs. The popes themselves have taken the lead in trying to make the Church native in every land.

As proof of this desire, a few years ago the Apostolic Delegate to China invited Fra Adelbert of Monte Cassino, an artist of distinction in the Beuronese style, to go to China and design churches in the Chinese style of art. Such churches, pictured in missionary magazines, are not lacking in Catholicity. In pictorial art, too, the representation of saints in the Chinese manner is no more strange than their painting by the Renaissance masters with Italian features and in Italian dress, even though, like the Apostles, they may have dwelt in the Holy Land. We think of Madonnas as traditional, even when not historically correct but mere attempts at local interpretation.

The *Catholic Art Bulletin* of October 28, 1927, published a letter from the Apostolic Delegate to China, Monsignor Celso Constantini, an authority on church architecture, on the subject of local development of religious art. We quote:

"All peoples have certain peculiar and well-defined characteristics that find their most solemn expression in architecture, which is the civil and social art *par excellence,* and which produces the historical monuments. These diverse artistic characteristics are the result of many factors: culture, customs, taste, historical and religious facts, materials of construction, climate, local temperature, etc.

"All history proves this: the great historic forms of art, Assyro-Chaldean, Egyptian, Greco-Roman, Byzantine, Gothic, all exhibit characters of entirely different peoples and epochs.

"Hence, it is an artistic blunder to import into this country the Roman and Gothic styles of Europe."

This is a fundamental principle which applies to other countries as well as to China.

The same idea was expressed by Dr. Downey, Archbishop of

INTERIOR, ST. JOSEPH'S CHURCH, SEATTLE, WASH.

A. H. Albertson, Architect, Seattle, Wash. Jos. W. Wilson and Paul Richardson, Associates

The rough surface similar to that of the exterior is a reminder of solidity and permanence. Such an interior does not call for much ornament, but there is a variety of color and contrast of light and shade.

[185]

Liverpool, in a letter published in *The Parthenon,* of London, England, January, 1932, in praise of the excellent cathedral under construction at Liverpool. The letter was as follows:

"There is a fascination about Sir Edwin Lutyen's design for the Metropolitan Cathedral at Liverpool. It is at first sight arresting and intriguing and holds one's attention by its indefinable charm. It is strong, it is bold, it is powerful, but it is also delicate, refined and subtle. It is obviously a holy place, a great temple, the house which has been builded for the great God Who claims the heavens as His throne and the earth as His footstool. Sir Edwin has given us something expressive of the religious spirit of our own day and generation instead of reproducing the temperament of bygone centuries. Each age has to restate ancient problems and solve them in new phraseology, and architecture, like painting or sculpture, to be sincere must reflect its period and, as it were, portray the throbbing life of the moment. It is as an interpreter of the thoughts and the feelings and the aspirations of many thousands on their knees in this the twentieth century that Sir Edwin has succeeded. His design satisfies the high requirement that a Cathedral be something not merely in which but with which to worship God.

Yours devotedly,

✠ Richard, Archbishop of Liverpool"

Other new churches in England show a tendency toward originality. The new chapel of the Charterhouse School, at Godalming in Surrey, a memorial to Carthusians who died in the War, was designed by Giles Gilbert Scott and is a departure from traditional Gothic design.

Maginnis and Walsh have made popular an adaptation of the Lombard style, a branch of the Romanesque used in north Italy. The original Lombard churches were somewhat crude in ornament but admirable in plan. The modernized style is well suited to modern construction and to rhythm of plan, as it allows wall space to be contrasted by window grouping of arcades.

A modernized Lombard style was first used in Rome about the beginning of this century. The church of St. Theresa in that style has a monastic severity of line and ornament. Other new churches show a tendency to break away from the overornamentation of the past. Santa Maria Liberatrice is quite modern, with Lombard ornament and angular lines. In place of a dome, at the crossing, we have here a square, suppressed tower. So, even in Rome we perceive the desire for living architecture. Although the Church is conservative in doctrine, yet she has always taken a lead in the search for beauty in newness. In other words, the Church is always modern. Truth is eternal, but social life has its brief span from day to day.

Modern Secular Architecture

Very few commercial structures are now erected in any ancient style. Skyscrapers built in recent times are all in the modern manner and have rejected the cornice and borrowed ornament. Since the World War the appearance of most city streets and skylines has been entirely changed by the new type of design. The general appearance has been greatly improved. Some few buildings give an impression of oddity, but the great majority are bright in color and pleasing in form. The new spirit is more than a passing fancy. It is based on fundamental principles and has produced a great improvement in American architecture.

The Church, then, must give some consideration to the prevailing type of design. If an American style is to be developed, the Church must give it some recognition. Churches being built now in ancient styles may in five years be hopelessly out of date. Therefore the question is quite practical. The Church need pay no attention to a passing fancy for some startling color or form, but if there is to be real improvement in design, churches are of sufficient importance to have the benefit of that progress.

[187]

ST. THOMAS THE APOSTLE CHURCH, CHICAGO, ILL.

Barry Byrne, Architect, Chicago, Ill.

Brick and terra cotta in logical construction. Rectangular window arches show the structural qualities of brick. The parapet is in accord with the plastic quality of terra cotta. Here is beauty without adherence to any traditional style.

MODERN ARCHITECTURE

Contemporary design is not to be considered a new style of architecture as a style has unyielding rules. The new method is merely logical construction adapted to place, purpose, and material. It represents the present rather than the past, but does not hate the past. Steel, glass, concrete, brick, and stone are employed, and each material is used in the way for which it is best suited. There is no useless ornament. Everything has a purpose. Vertical and horizontal lines predominate. Circles, squares, and triangles are planned to produce contrast. Everything is exact and geometrical. Windows are grouped so as to leave large masses of unbroken wall. High buildings are set back at the top, having something of the form of a pyramid. Others are a cluster of structures rising to various heights. Although classical in simplicity, some of the new buildings have almost as much variety of outline as an ancient Gothic cathedral.

There is a new admiration of material in its natural state. Steel ribs are not disguised. Wood is not painted and carved to represent iron or other material; it is respected for its own merits. Terra cotta is not used to imitate marble or stone. It is a lawful building material and need not be disguised. Its variety of color, facility of being molded, and lowness of cost are advantages. Brick is produced in such a variety of colors that its utility and beauty have been remarkably increased. String courses and geometric designs in varicolored brick show the touch of an artist. Flat, monotonous walls are a thing of the unlamented past.

In furnishings the same geometric lines are observed; plain mass, bordered by straight lines. Bright colors of woven texture give relief to what would otherwise be formal atmosphere. Texture is admired and unusual weaves are sought. Wood is not painted nor carved. Beauty of grain and natural colors are preserved by wax instead of varnish or paint. In this the modernists (a name for today which must be changed tomorrow) seem to have improved in sincerity even over the ancient classical builders. The Greeks, noted for logical construction, used polychrome decoration on wood and even on carved marble. There is reason to believe that the frieze of the Parthenon at Athens, although carved by a master hand, was once ornamented in colors. In later styles, carved ornament of wood and marble has been poly-chromed and critics have sometimes wondered if it were proper, but use by the masters was considered sufficient authority. They used color, not to disguise the material, but to add to its beauty. But now it is considered more proper to leave material in its natural state and, with that in mind, material is chosen for its texture and innate beauty. Iron, however, is enameled, as that is considered a lawful finish for metal.

Shall the Church Go Modernistic?

Many of the new reforms in construction are exactly the im-provements for which a few churchmen have been clamoring — logical construction, brighter colors, less ornament, and no dis-guising of material. Some, therefore, recommend the adoption of the new style in the design of churches. In fact, it has been used for a considerable number of new Catholic churches in France, and especially in Germany. But the new designs, so far, have only novelty to recommend them. In Spain, the new cathedral of Bar-celona is entirely original in style. The spires we there behold might have been as appealing as Gothic, but they fail in beauty and in grace of design, and we should not like to consider this edifice as the first of a series in that style. The new churches of Germany have broken away entirely from the past. They use geometric lines without domes or pinnacles. The cross is the only reminder of their purpose. Leaving off the cross, the buildings could be used for any secular purpose.

We wanted change and it has come. Here, then, is the prob-lem. Should we follow the leadership of those who seek logical construction but novelty of form, or shall we adopt structural principles which are not new but newly recognized, and thus develop a style of our own?

ENTRANCE DETAIL, ST. THOMAS THE APOSTLE CHURCH,
CHICAGO, ILL.

Barry Byrne, Architect, Chicago, Ill.

Logical planning requires a different kind of building for a church than for a theater or office building. There is no reason why church architecture should not be in a class by itself. That principle is approved by the moderns, as they wish to do away with styles and periods of art.

It is true that there may not be unrestrained individualism in churches, since they must be in harmony with other structures in the neighborhood. We must, at least, modify our designs for the sake of harmony. If we do not build in the new style, we must be conscious of its presence and follow the popular taste for simplicity and strength. Logical planning and construction were always important, but they are more so now.

Yet commerce and factories do not hold us back, as a highly artistic sense of beauty has recently developed in spite of them. But our churches are retarded by years of indifference to the worthiness of their high purpose. Office buildings and railroad stations represent their purpose; most churches do not. Revivals of the past have failed because too much attention was given to historical detail and to ornament. Now, there is an age of great construction at hand because, for the first time in many centuries, *more attention is paid to structure than to ornament.*

The new structures are said to represent a materialistic, mechanical age. There is no such intention in the minds of the builders, but architecture does represent the age. It cannot be avoided. Even when a Gothic church is built to represent another age, machine-age methods are used in carving wood and stone and polishing marble. The mark of the time cannot be avoided except by deliberate and painstaking effort. So, an age of time-saving methods is represented by modern building as an accidental quality.

But the spirit of the Church is different. The Church is not only of today. It is rooted in the past and is ever mindful of the future. The new style, therefore, cannot be used by the Church without adaptation. The Church may use the vertical and horizontal lines, and the unbroken wall masses of the new architecture, but must add to it figures suggestive of God, the soul, and eternal life. Unadorned building material cannot do this. It must be done by symbolism. The formal beauty of classical art is earthly, not spiritual. Beauty is a pleasure of sense and does not necessarily elevate the soul to spiritual striving. The most admirable combination of geometric exactness will not make a church. It has been used in the service of religion, but it must first be consecrated. Marble and precious wood were made by the Creator, but when used in a building their first suggestion is of the wonderful works of man. To make certain of the suggestion of the worship of God there must be added references, in symbolic design and pictures, that will call to mind the presence of God and the history and tradition of His Church.

The Gothic style was an imitation of nature and therefore it raised the soul to the worship of the Creator of nature. A geometric design without symbolism is entirely the work of man. It ignores nature and, therefore, God. We cannot use a modernistic design for a church, without recourse to the proper adaptation. But we are not prevented from availing ourselves of the new style if we combine with its rectangles a certain amount of symbolic decoration. In doing so, we should merely be following a modern principle — suitability to purpose and logical construction. So, by starting an independent school of our own, we may build churches in a new style, with straight lines and large wall masses and plain surfaces; with natural wood, concrete, and steel beams, representative of the age and in harmony with the office buildings and residences that surround them — but somewhere we must break the wall surface with statues, paintings, or carved relief which signify more than the mere material can ever represent.

It is quite possible to respect tradition and yet be modern. We can be reminded of the soul and yet be at home in a mechanical civilization. The Church is adaptable to any circumstance as it was intended for all times. The dominion of God and the empire of Cæsar are separate entities, yet God's Church is on Cæsar's earth. Christ reminded His hearers of their obligations toward both kingdoms. The Church cannot do Christ's work on earth by proclaiming a lack of interest in the present — by insisting on a return to thirteenth-century conditions. Time does not move backward. The past is interesting and admirable, but it is past. The invention of machinery and the organization of big business may have been a mistake, but we cannot return to hand labor, individual independence, and town government. It is the duty of the Church to teach people how to live in present conditions. This can be done, not by rebelling against that which is praiseworthy, but by the consecration of modern life to the service of God.

An important step in spiritual progress is learning how to use material things for our spiritual benefit. In this modern world we cannot follow the soulless methods of a purely commercial art, but we may use new building material in a new way. We should not imitate, but lead out in a new direction. The new building art may in a manner be compared with that of the ancient Greeks. The Church has never been able to use Greek architecture, partly because there was no historical connection and partly because Greek temples did not stir the imagination. The Greeks sought beauty of line and attained it. There could be no more progress but only repetition. There was beauty, it is true, but pagan, fatalistic beauty — cold and dead. The low, flat ceiling and the straight lines were considered oppressive by the early Christians. In the Roman basilica, the ceiling could be raised in a clerestory, but even that improvement was not satisfactory until the development of Romanesque, and finally came the Gothic vaults. But now, in adopting a geometric, horizontal style, we are not limited by stone construction. We can raise the flat ceiling to an imposing height and even the rectangular windows, high, narrow, and rhythmically grouped, may raise the soul heavenward by perpendicular lines as powerfully as the Gothic style, although in a manner that is new.

Ruskin would have the builders of his time avoid the use of iron and build only in stone, using the logic of stone construction even if other material were employed. But the world has moved on. Stone buildings themselves, if we may call them so, are only faced with stone. Instead of stone walls, ten or twelve feet thick, commercial buildings have structural frames of welded steel — a cheaper, faster, and more pliable method than stone construction. The support of weight and thrusts is thus solved in a new manner. We cannot hold back progress in construction. We need only see that it remains logical.

A fifty-story building in stone would be impossible, or at least dangerous, as each stone would be an independent unit. It would be almost out of the question to find builders, at present, who could construct a church roof of stone. Medieval Gothic builders constructed the ribs of the vaulting first and then filled in the intervening space. Some of the vaults fell in before they were finished. It was difficult work and required great skill and careful planning. We admire the ability of those great artisans and the beauty of the final result, but there are better methods now and we need not keep to the old merely because it is old. A stone vault must of necessity have a narrow span, making the nave narrow. But new methods enable us to build a ceiling to any width we may desire and accordingly the nave may be logically widened.

Stone is not a more religious material than brick, concrete, steel, or glass. The religious atmosphere comes from the manner in which all these are used. Some ancient churches, carefully planned and as carefully erected with great engineering skill, are less inspiring than other churches not so correct in structure. The churches which inspire the beholder are those which we find to be more imaginative in their plan and ornament, and more reverent in their manner. Organic plan and logical construction are important for churches as well as for secular buildings, but added to those good qualities the church must possess reverence. That was once admirably attained in stone, but it is unreasonable to claim it cannot be attained with any other material. Not the material, but the way in which it is used betokens the spirit.

Let us, then, make clear this one point. *A church may be built of any material, with any method of honest construction, in any style of design, old or new, but preferably a new one or an original variation of an old one, provided only it attain the first purpose of a church — to give honor and glory to God.*

If that seems a simple requirement, stop to think of how many churches have been built to honor a certain nation, a king, or a city, or perhaps the architect and artists rather than God.

Even the builders of some of the truly great ancient churches might be accused of a slight degree of vanity for building steeples too high or too numerous, and for making the West Front more beautiful and pretentious than justified by the interior or the rest of the exterior. Modern efficiency and directness would never be guilty of those faults.

"Form and Reform"

A recent book on modern art and architecture, *Form and Reform,* by Paul T. Frankl (Harpers, 1930), may be considered as an authoritative summary of the principles of modern painting and building from an American point of view. The author objects to schools of art and pleads for individualism. Following our own inclinations, let us reject what is unattractive in the new art and accept what is admirable. The general movement is unruly, but within it is a group which tends toward classical simplicity. Ignoring the irregular and the unnatural, we may select certain of their principles, on which we may establish something suitable for the Church. Or else, entirely ignoring their principles, we may in some few cases approve of the final result and build something somewhat similar, founded on principles exactly the opposite. Nothing modern is to be copied without modification, for to copy modern work is no less objectionable than to copy ancient art.

The use of wood in its natural beauty might be adopted. We have employed wood, painted, gilded, and carved beyond recognition. The finest wood is given a coat of varnish which puts it in the same class with that which is the most common. Mere lumber is stained to represent rare wood. One of our favorite desecrations has been the painting of wooden altars in imitation of marble. By a few strokes of the brush we bring the most precious marble from its far-off quarries. Most of our wood carving is uninteresting and lacking the artistic touch because it is done easily by machinery.

So much deception has been practised that people rarely take an interest in any object of wood, as they do not expect to find anything of quality or artistic merit. Marble is a better material for altars, but if we use wood, why disguise it? A better plan would be to preserve its natural beauty by a coat of wax. A block of beautifully grained wood has sufficient virtue in itself. Man cannot improve on it by painting or varnishing.

The same holds true of marble. If the carving only were desirable, then wood, as more easily carved, could best answer this purpose. But marble, coming from the earth as God made it, has its own natural beauty. Carved ornament in familiar designs, done in factory style by machinery, can add nothing to its beauty but may destroy all the reminders of its natural origin. Let us have marble unadorned. It need not always be white. Good results have been obtained by the use of buff-colored, unpolished Minnesota marble, similar to Caen stone from France. A small amount of carving of some religious symbol is a reminder of the high purpose of the altar. To cover it with meaningless carving would hide the fact that it is marble — nature's masterpiece.

If we cannot afford marble, why imitate it? Concrete is a lawful building material, but imitation marble is not. Concrete may be colored and offers unlimited opportunity for various color schemes. The material need not be designed to represent something else. Let it stand on its own merit. Colored concrete is used by the modernists to good effect and we must admire their honesty in not veining it to represent marble. Of course, a consecrated altar must be of natural stone, but most American altars are "portable altars," that is, they have a consecrated altar stone in the center and the rest of the altar may be of any material.

Tapestries and rich cloth hangings are a part of the new art. They are appropriate as altar screens or canopies. They improve acoustics and give warmth and homelikeness to the interior.

The new art is the emphasis of material rather than form. In all past art even the rarest marble has been ornamentally carved. Perhaps the modernists are unconsciously coming nearer to nature and to God when they hold it needless to ornament marble, wood, and woven cloth. The perfection of material in the ornamentation of a church may be a thank offering to God more fitting than the feeble artistic work of man. But, as previously stated, there must be enough ornament in religious symbols to show the consecration of the material to the service of God.

In the new method, beauty of outline is not sought; the outline suggests only the functional purpose of the building. This principle would require that a church be devotional in appearance and allowance is thereby made for the separate development of church architecture, as its purpose is entirely different from commercial and domestic architecture.

Introduction of Modern Architecture

In the summer of 1925 the International Exposition of Decorative Arts was held in Paris. It introduced modern architecture to a surprised world. Little had been said about it before and it was strange that the Exposition now showed the same tendencies to be developed in all European countries and even in Japan. Abbé Dimnet called the new adventure "that hopelessly superannuated thing 'modern style.'" It had been in existence for thirty years as the *"Art Nouveau"* movement, but was limited to decoration. Now it began to be used in the building arts.

The Exposition was supposed to be international, but America was not invited to take part, as American art was not noted for startling effects. For that we are thankful. It nullifies any accusation that may be made against American design by conservative Americans. Novelty of design does not put us in the revolutionary class, since the leaders of the new movement rejected American art as too conservative. It is a strange situation. Americans are blamed for the "jazz age" as represented by modern dances, music, and moving pictures. At the same time, while all the rest of the world is going to extremes in art, America preserves the classical spirit.

In 1925 certain so-called modern buildings had been erected in our larger cities, and the vertical note of the structures in the Paris Exposition came from America. Some European architects and artists look to the American architect Frank Lloyd Wright as the founder of the modern movement, but in Europe the principles were carried to extremes while Americans clung to logic and beauty. Europeans seek novelty merely as a protest against war and poverty. They wish to forget the past. Americans are less inclined to protest. They do not feel helpless as individuals and have never been driven to anarchy by political or social conditions. Since architecture expresses the character of a people, it is a hopeful sign to have American architecture rejected by the radicals. National individuality may thus have an opportunity to be developed. We need no longer depend on Europe for art leadership. We have grown up and can take care of ourselves.

CHURCH ARCHITECTURE

Modern Churches in Germany

Our purpose is not to copy in our own land the work of another country or even of another city, but we may have something to learn by the study of what others are at present doing. Architecture is a series of experiments, and if someone else has tried out a certain building material or a certain form, we may profitably consider the results of his experiment.

The new architecture is said to be irreligious and to represent a materialistic age. It is so only because that is the spirit of the age. Lack of spirituality is not a principle of modern architecture, yet a godless designer will unconsciously show his lack of faith in the work he produces. A devout man using the same style will as readily show his reverence without special effort.

France and Spain have made several attempts at church building in the new style, but it has been used more extensively in Germany. Among the least extreme of the experiments made there we may count the St. Peter Canisius Church in Friedrichshafen. The entrance portal is a group of three high round arches. Above the arches is a Crucifixion group. At first glance the façade might seem to be a false front, which would be bad architecture, but it is more than a wall; it is deep enough to contain a belfry and is set back in rectangular lines. The sanctuary of the church is a single pointed arch with a high cross above the simple altar.

An interesting feature of many new churches is the use of concrete for ceilings. By the construction of forms in various ways the concrete has been molded into interesting designs. Ceilings are flat with parallel lines, round arch or pointed arch, vaulted with ornamental lines in quarries, circles, diamonds, or parallel lines.

Christ the King Church, in Zofingen, has shallow transepts, not rectangular but circular in form. The altar railing is curved to continue the circle. St. Paul's Church, in Göttingen, displays a sanctuary in circular form, with a curved Communion rail com-

INTERIOR, ST. HENRY'S CHURCH, BAMBERG, GERMANY

Professor Michael Kurz, Architect, Augsburg, Germany

Reinforced concrete in logical design. The ceiling is of Lamella wood construction, which wastes no space and is pleasing in design. In the completed church the Communion railing and the sanctuary walls form a circle. The upward soaring arches have the inspiring effect of Gothic vaults in a new interpretation.

pleting the circle. Others have high narrow windows classical in the severity of their angles. St. Anthony Church, in Schneidemuhl, presents a new treatment of skylight or dome. It consists of four concentric receding circles. The light entering at the center produces a spiritual splendor, but the effect is spoiled by a large crucifix in modern design, like an atheistic Russian cartoon. A church near Cologne is portable being made of glass with steel frames. It is interesting only for its novelty. Copper and other metals are used for ornament of exteriors and interiors.

A hospital, in Münster, Germany, has on one end of the building a statue, thirty feet high, of the Blessed Virgin Mary. It was desired to avoid great weight on account of sandy soil so a lightly constructed roof was covered with copper and the statue was made of wood covered with ordinary sheet copper. The process is thus described in the *Bulletin of the Copper and Brass Research Association* (Oct. 1, 1931): "A full-size model was made by a sculptor as the base for the copper work. This was reinforced by oak wood and was divided into horizontal rings. The copper sheet was fitted over this model by hammering and was riveted at the seams, which correspond to the horizontal rings. The copper is fastened to these rings."

In the beginning of this chapter we urged the need of originality. Without doubt, the new churches in Germany have it. But that is not enough. Many of the features mentioned in the foregoing are admirable. All designers may learn something from their excellent handling of ceiling design. The possibility of molding concrete into various forms makes it a material especially desirable for ceiling construction. The ancient Romans used it for domes, but now its superior quality gives a possibility of other forms. And yet the new churches of Germany are not altogether admirable. Painted and carved ornament in the modernistic style has broken away from all tradition and therefore has no religious suggestion. The churches represent the despair of post-war poverty and unrest. A flat, bare wall is neither beautiful nor religious. If it has any symbolism, it signifies despair. But a church must suggest its religious purpose, which is done by painted and carved symbols or pictures. The architectural lines in many churches have the simplicity and dignity of a Greek temple, but they lack the consecration to God. If decorated in the Beuron style, the churches would be more beautiful and certainly more devotional.

Experiments made in churches of Germany and other countries with painting in modernistic style have failed. It does not produce a religious atmosphere. The difficulty in Germany is the same as that experienced during past years in the United States — the need of artists. A structural engineer may design an attractive building without having remarkable artistic ability, but only an artist can decorate the interior. And real artists are not numerous.

In structure most of the German churches are admirable. The interior form represents the wall structure. Ceiling and roof are a unit. In some, however, there are straight walls and a plain pitch roof, while the interior has a false ceiling and false walls. In such cases the interior appearance may be good, but the structure is bad. It is like the lath-and-plaster vaulting of American churches of the past generation. We have here an easy way of arriving at effects, but it is not suited to church construction where everything should be what it pretends to be. False ceilings and attics are no longer needed to keep out heat in summer and cold in winter, since insulating material will now produce the effect.

The disapproval of the new style in churches, expressed by several members of the German hierarchy, was based on the lack of spirituality and reverence rather than on novelty of outline. To be unchurchlike is an unpardonable fault in a church. In some cases the fault is in the interior furnishings and decoration, or lack of them. Others followed false principles and were not intended to appear law-abiding.

An interesting form of wooden ceiling arch, occupying little space and pleasing in appearance, was invented in Germany. An example is the St. Henry's Church in Bamberg. Like the fan vaulting in English late Gothic ceilings, the arch is divided into small geometric branches which cover the entire ceiling and support it. No attic is required and full use of interior space is allowed. This form of construction is not so unsightly as wood trusses and is much lighter than steel or concrete. It is coming into use in this country for wide spans, such as airplane hangars, and is known here as "Lamella Trussless Wood Roof Construction." It may be fireproofed on the underside with plaster board and above with fireproof shingles.

As a lesson to be drawn from architectural experiments in Germany and elsewhere we may say that the better designs correspond fairly well to what we actually desire in modern church construction, but there is need of more ornament on the exterior and a better balance of composition. For the interior we must have more color and ornament as well as a more religious spirit.

Other Concrete Churches

In Prague a new concrete church has recently been erected in which the roof rises by steps, reaching its greatest height at the sanctuary end. This gives elevation and dignity to the sanctuary by the comparison it suggests, a method used in ancient basilicas to give comparative height to the nave. In the case of the Prague church, windows have further been inserted in the risers of the roof steps, thus shedding light from the rear and from above in the daytime, and producing an interesting effect in its exterior view at night by the illumination within. Still other windows are placed in the sanctuary and tower.

Another church of concrete built at Vincennes, Paris, has an

CHURCH IN VINCENNES, PARIS

Reproduced from "Architectural Design in Concrete" with permission of the
Oxford Press, by courtesy of Ernest Benn Limited.

Concrete structure with brick surface, giving only a hint of the wide
span of interior arches. In the ancient Byzantine churches, concrete
would sustain no bending pressure, and the domes were supported
by heavy piers. Now a wide and graceful arch is possible, and the
interior is left unobstructed.

ST. PASCAL'S CHURCH, CHICAGO, ILL.

Raymond Gregori, Architect, Chicago, Ill.

The windows are new in design. The entrance arch with the crucifix is unique, majestic, and suggestive of the purpose of the building. It gives depth to the front elevation. The rectangular lines of the panels on the side are a logical use of brick. The tower, unbroken at the base and ornamented at the top, is powerful and beautiful. It has depth and variety and the set-back finial is a concession to modern taste. Almost hidden by the tower is a chimney, ornamental as well as useful.

exterior surface of brick with window traceries of concrete. The
ground plan is like that of many ancient Byzantine churches —
a Greek cross within a square. The church is topped by a half
dome. The interior is a remote reminder of Hagia Sophia, with
its wide auditorium and great sweep of arches, but in the Paris
church the arches are more prominent. Some of these are round
and others pointed. Such a church, molded in a single unit, has
a massive impressiveness not possible of attainment by brick or
stone. But concrete needs decoration. The soffits of the arches are
in colors and there are medallions painted on the walls, leaving
the rough concrete texture as a background. In such structures
stone arches may logically be ornamented by carving and concrete arches may have some painted decoration, since the undecorated portion shows the material to be genuine.

Logical construction in concrete naturally calls for wide spans
or arches rather than for the Basilican clerestory. In the basilica,
marble pillars could not be high, and so arose the need of a second story, starting from the level of the side-aisle roof, to make
the central nave higher. But with concrete construction, the arch
can without difficulty span the full width of the church and
there is no need of pillars. Height, dignity, and solemnity can be
attained by wide-sweeping monolithic arches, a form of construction now returning to favor. But it was already used by ancient Rome and Constantinople. Stone cannot span a wide space
but concrete can.

Another peculiarity of concrete is the possibility of lofty vertical structure which it affords. Marble, stone, or brick piers, pillars,
or arches must be limited in height or built with a carefully calculated system of balance and counter-thrusts, as in Gothic structure. But concrete-and-steel construction allows great height, as
in modern skyscrapers. Few experiments have been made with
churches in that method, but it obviously contains possibilities of
impressiveness by unusual height in nave or sanctuary. This

INTERIOR, ST. PASCAL'S CHURCH, CHICAGO, ILL.

Raymond Gregori, Architect, Chicago, Ill.

Good proportion and balance. Continuous side walls with openings to give depth and contrast.

would give a Gothic effect in a new kind of structure. Some of the German churches have a hint of the upward soaring effect from high, parallel columns. But there are possibilities of still greater development of that spirit.

In the churches at LeRaincy and St. Denis in Paris the walls have been molded in concrete, with ornamental perforations, like ancient Roman perforated windows. But the experiment of practically turning all the walls into windows is not satisfactory. It was done in Gothic structure, as in the Sainte Chapelle of Paris, but there the structural ribs are more in evidence. In the concrete churches just mentioned, structure is ignored and no balance of window and wall mass exists to convey the impression of repose. If used with the old Greek proportion of two to three, there are great possibilities of beauty in concrete perforated windows.

Concrete is adaptable to beauty of ornament, as it may be easily molded into various forms. Variety may be given after the forms have been removed and before the concrete sets, and it may be easily chiseled into ornamental designs after it has set. This gives a possibility of symbolic emblems in relief on exterior and interior walls. There is a further possibility of having variety of texture by chiseling off the smooth surface on some portions of the wall and leaving the rough aggregate exposed for contrast. Colors may be introduced by using aggregates of various colors and experiments are now being made with dyes.

The advantage of concrete at present is the same advantage that had already been discovered by the ancient Romans — the possibility of securing strong and artistic structure with common labor under proper supervision. It is not the best building material, but it is lower in cost than stone and better in effect than brick, while it holds possibilities of structure and artistic effect not found in any other material. If designers, using that material, have turned away from traditional styles, they have

[209]

RECTORY AND CHURCH OF THE HOLY CHILD JESUS, RICHMOND HILL, BROOKLYN, N. Y.

Henry V. Murphy, Architect, Brooklyn, N. Y.

The walls are in orange-shaded brick trimmed with stone. Rectangular lines proper for brick construction.
Good balance of wall mass and windows. The front has depth and interesting variety. The tower has charm
and is a good center of gravity.

done so not in contempt nor in a revolutionary spirit, but to suit the peculiar structural qualities of the material. If, unintentionally, concrete construction of churches has up to the present represented a machine age, it has failed to serve the end we must have in view. There is need of development away from factory construction toward greater beauty, majesty, and reverence. Our best efforts are to be offered not to commerce but to God.

Modern American Churches

Several concrete churches exist in America. Noteworthy among them is the new St. Joseph's Church in Seattle, Washington, in charge of the Jesuit Order. It is built entirely of concrete; walls, roof, floor, and tower constitute one solid monolith. To make provision for the inevitable expansion and contraction, expansion joints were left at intervals, but hidden from sight. Still further to prevent an excessive expansion due to the sun's heat, the roof was covered with insulating material. A dampproof material was mixed with the concrete and a coat of dampproofing paint was applied on the exterior walls in a light-tan stone color.

A description of the church was given in *The Architect and Engineer* of San Francisco, for February, 1931. The lines of the building are naturally rectangular. Little ornament is used. There are some painted symbols on ceiling beams, arches, pulpit, and dome. "Character and quality were sought by the use of proportion, color, and light, by the influence of lines, the relation of surfaces, the relative values of voids and masses." The altars are of marble with mosaic ornament. The Stations of the Cross are also of mosaic. Stained-glass windows of subdued colors are to be added later. The transepts have a lower roof than the nave, leaving the lines of the nave continuous, but contrasted by the openings. The rough markings of the wooden forms are seen on the concrete surface. Even the pulpit is of concrete. Unless brightened by color, gray concrete walls would appear cold, so warmth of color was introduced by painting the interior in "a faintly rusty and neutral wine color, with a suggestion of tarnished silver underneath."

The Stations are described as "of archaic design." This, we hope, does not mean primitive and distorted, since formal and conventional design should preserve some objective reality. Otherwise it does not aid devotion. In this case we trust to the good taste of the designer.

Another concrete church on the West Coast is Precious Blood Church in Los Angeles, erected in the modernized Lombard style. The interior is traditional in treatment, but the exterior, with its decoration in relief, shows the suitability of concrete to church ornament.

St. Vincent's Church, in Los Angeles, constructed in a modern variation of the Spanish Renaissance style, shows the suitability of concrete to molded ornament.

Several non-Catholic churches have been erected in concrete as well as many schools and public and commercial buildings. Reference could be made to some of them, if necessary, but the churches mentioned show all the desirable structural and ornamental qualities of concrete — its suitability to great height, great width of span, variety of texture, molded and carved ornament, strength, unity, and a spirit of monastic austerity, classic simplicity, or medieval romanticism.

Modern builders have neither the time nor the patience to build in the Gothic style, balancing stone on stone. Churches which we call Gothic display a wooden ceiling or one faced with tile, both of which features are illogical in construction. Concrete may be used logically without great cost and at the same time has capabilities of beauty of ornament. There are, in fact, unlimited possibilities of variety in ceiling ribs. Forms used for concrete in one place may be slightly changed for the sake of variety when moved to another portion of the ceiling. And even flamboyant ornament would not add greatly to the cost. It would be an offering of the mind rather than of the purse.

There is no demand that all new churches be of concrete and independent of the past. But with the possibilities of creative art thus clearly set before us, we should no longer feel bound here in loyalty to the past. Copied beauty is better than ugliness and vulgarity, but far inferior to original beauty. An effort to make each church a creative offering to the Supreme Creator will open up a field of "Catholic Action" closed for many centuries.

The possibility of originality is especially inviting at the present time. Brick and stone have structural limitations, but concrete has more extensive usefulness, even though modern concrete churches have not as yet been noted for their devotional atmosphere. Great progress, however, has been made in structure. We may learn from the experiments of others. The field is open for a designer who will plan a church, original in design, logical in structure, and at the same time beautiful in exterior and interior appearance, while prayerful in atmosphere.

Here, then, is an opportunity to serve Christ and His Church no less great than that which presented itself to Constantine when he planned the first basilica, or to Abbot Lanfranc when he dreamed of Gothic arches, or to Michelangelo when, in a new style, he designed a cathedral for the world. It is an opportunity and a challenge rarely given in the long and glorious history of church architecture.

We do not expect all new churches to be in the modern style. Some will be so situated in parish groups that it will be necessary to match them carefully with buildings already existing, but old styles may be adapted to a modern, or let us rather say, a contemporary design. If a few churches, recognized as meritorious by architects and people of good taste can be erected, then the many unimaginative designs hitherto produced can readily be overlooked.

INTERIOR, CHURCH OF THE HOLY CHILD JESUS, RICHMOND HILL, BROOKLYN, N. Y.

Henry V. Murphy, Architect, Brooklyn, N. Y.

The same kind of brick and stone as on the exterior. Variety of breaks in the side walls. Polychrome ceiling. Sanctuary arch and altar well proportioned. No forced striving for beauty.

ENTRANCE, CHURCH OF THE HOLY CHILD JESUS, RICHMOND
HILL, BROOKLYN, N. Y.

Henry V. Murphy, Architect, Brooklyn, N. Y.

[215]

We must admit that concrete, as an ornamental structural material, is still in its experimental stage. Bridges and other structures, after standing twenty years, show discoloration, cracking, and surface crumbling. But limestone at that age needs cleaning and a brick wall must be painted. Old concrete which was carefully made has withstood the weather. That which deteriorated had faults at the start. It was intended only to support great weight, and did that well. Little thought was given to its appearance. Now that concrete has an ornamental as well as a structural purpose it is necessary to use more care in the mixing. Materials must be clean and regular in quality, and the surface must be free of gravel pockets, which would give the weather an opening wedge. In the Seattle church such pockets were chiseled out and filled. A weatherproof coat was further ground into the surface by a revolving carborundum disk, without destroying the watermarks and the marks of the forms. More care is now required with the surface in the making. Not all concrete is good, but it can be made good.

Objectors will conclude immediately that the use of concrete means modernistic design. The conclusion is not justified. We may ignore the modernistic movement and still use concrete in a new manner of structure. Modernistic design tried elsewhere for churches has failed, except insofar as it shows others a way of improvement. But the Church is not interested in attempting the mechanization of the spirit. At the very time when modern standardization is showing its inability to keep workmen from starving, plans are being made to extend factory efficiency to the home — to have houses built in sections and set up in a few hours; to have cooking, heating, cleaning, and janitor work managed by a syndicate. Fabricated metals would reduce the cost of building and large-scale supervision would reduce the cost of operation. Yet everyone knows that, under such a régime, when the bills arrive they will be twice as large as previously. The whole idea is a respectably horrible one, like a Greek tragedy. It would take all the joy out of life. We do not need more organization but more democracy, more individual effort.

In the past our churches have been standardized. We wish them to be individual creative efforts. If concrete and new synthetic metals and insulating material are to be used in churches of the future, that by itself will be no reason for calling them modernistic churches. The Church is not in sympathy with soulless capitalism. She has ever been equally opposed to slavery at the one extreme and anarchy at the other, particularly when there is question of things of the mind; and she has not changed that policy.

Such, in brief, is the situation. The conservatives live in the past. They are the Byzantines, making exact and unchanging rules for church art, which of old invented new styles, but must never do so again.

Then comes the insane group of modernists, men who would forget the past and live in the future. Like all the mentally unbalanced, they are given to seeing visions which are unreal, ugly, and incoherent.

Next we have the sane-minded class, those who truly live in the present and with sound logic adapt their materials to new methods and conditions.

The Church can never lock step with either extreme, whether of the Left or of the Right. She belongs, by instinct and tradition, to the Center party.

Modern Groups

Try as they may to avoid working in "styles," contemporary architects are gathered naturally into groups according to their system of thought. A design is a product of the mind and must be influenced by the esthetic principles of the designer. A discussion of the various groups will be helpful. It cannot be complete

CHURCH OF THE MOST PRECIOUS BLOOD,
LONG ISLAND CITY, N. Y.

Henry J. McGill, Architect, New York, N. Y.

Of seam-faced granite. The small amount of ornament and the lack of cornice
show the hardness of granite. At the top of the robust tower is the early
Christian symbol of immortality — peacocks at the fountain of life. The entire
composition suggests perpetuity.

[218]

INTERIOR, CHURCH OF THE MOST PRECIOUS BLOOD,
LONG ISLAND CITY, N. Y.

Henry J. McGill, Architect, New York, N. Y.

Modern in spirit but not extreme. Geometric lines. A new treatment of altar
canopy, suspended from the ceiling. Stations of the Cross and other fixtures
were especially designed. The interior is attractive artistically and spiritually.

[219]

SIDE VIEW, CHURCH OF THE MOST PRECIOUS BLOOD, LONG ISLAND CITY, N. Y.

Henry J. McGill, Architect, New York, N. Y.

Treated in brick and stone trim to harmonize with a rectory, previously built, to which the new church was joined. A good combination of brick and stone. Water spouts and other metal work are of white nonstaining metal.

and exact any more than can the grouping of ancient architects and artists into schools. But a loose classification of groups will help us to understand present tendencies. We arrange them as follows according to the architectural feature which they consider most important.

Interior Space

Frank Lloyd Wright is the leader of this group. Judging from his *Autobiography*,[1] and from his work, he considers the walls of all previous buildings "prisonlike." He wishes wide, flat roofs to give a sense of shelter. A great deal of glass is used in walls to make them less confining in appearance, and windows turn corners to avoid the inclusive strength of walls. Only the interior matters and the walls follow the arrangement of rooms with no external ornament, no balance of form, and no effort to please the eye. There is cold efficiency — the utility of a skeleton to support the body, but beauty is not produced and not desired. Wright considers a building not only representative of the machine age but a machine in itself.

These ideas have been used to a greater extent in Germany than in America. The style (for it deserves the name) has not met with approval except by those who accept its fundamental principles. But the designers in this method do not seek approval. It is a style of utility and is interesting as is anything new, but it purposely rejects tried structural principles and takes nothing from the past. But even the builder of a factory has social obligations. His building should have advertising value and should add to the good appearance of the neighborhood and of the city.

This style is often called "functional," as each portion of the design is based on utility. Ruskin wrote a great deal about function but this is a new interpretation of it. The term "International Style" has also been applied to it.

---

[1] Longmans, Green & Co.

This group makes common use of concrete, which is a "fluid" medium and can be poured into any shape of mold. But we have shown in text and illustrations that concrete has nobler uses than mere utility and unity of mass. It may also be ornamental.

Yet there was need of a revolution. The modernists accomplished a great deal for the general benefit of architecture by calling attention to the need of creative design. In this country they broke the control of the humanists who would recognize nothing but Greek and Roman design. The only stronghold left to paganism is in government buildings, but that line was broken by the excellent new State Capitol at Lincoln, Nebraska, which is a victory for creative American architecture.

Surface Beauty

Early American skyscrapers used Gothic or classical details without consideration for structure or form. Pleasing effects were accidental, as they were not based on logic. A group at the present time insists on external beauty alone without consideration for material or structure. As a result of the prevailing good taste such designers may by chance produce some good-looking buildings, but they are adding nothing to the science of architecture. Efforts not based on fundamental principles cannot long continue in government, religion, business, or art.

Form

This group does not believe in ornament. Its members seek beauty only in the balanced proportion of parts. They go further for beauty than the functionalists, who would not vary the outline an inch to make a better composition and who place windows for utility without consideration for the general plan. Those who seek beauty in form pay little attention to structure. Within this group are those who build false fronts. The outer appearance is designed first and the structure fills in the inner space. Like the surface-beauty group, it arrives at results by a short cut of reasoning and cannot contribute anything of permanent value.

Structure Alone

Throughout all architectural history, the structural qualities of material used had an influence on the design of the building. Structural engineers have come recently into prominence because of the large size and height of commercial buildings. Some architects have been satisfied to be only structural engineers. The first setback buildings were like piles of boxes without composition or ornament. This did not last long as it was unsatisfactory to the sight. Public opinion demanded adornment.

Structure and Form

This is the logical style. Just as the Greek, basing everything on reason, was the most perfect of ancient styles, so the best American architects have accomplished wonders in the past few years by the application of reason to building plans. Long ago, thinkers tried to show logical structure in skyscrapers by vertical ribs to represent the steel skeleton. Later the skeleton became a single unit welded together. Ribs were no longer of importance, but rectangular sections were grouped together in mass proportion, and ornament was used for variety and interest. Simultaneously our cities took on a new appearance with structures powerful as the pyramids of Egypt and proportion of mass and embellishment, not indeed as refined in detail, but as distinctive in general effect as anything produced by ancient Greece or Rome. We need no longer apologize for the poverty of American art. Our new buildings represent the power, organization, courage, and good humor of our people. For the first time our architecture is representative of the genius of the nation.

On this subject, *Architecture,* for March, 1932, quoted Donald R. Dohner, Director of Art in the Engineering Department of the Westinghouse Electric and Manufacturing Company as follows:

"Modern art is a sensible art — a utilitarian art, an engineering art. Much has been heard of the 'modern manner,' worse still, the 'modernistic.' Much has been made of queer angles, zigzag lines, childish color schemes, 'galloping gazelles' — all this is thought of as modern. This is modernistic; it is the mannerism of cheap faddists.

"But the real and vital art, the art that is modern, is the art reflecting our contemporary life. It is an art that grows out of and is related to our needs, our materials and methods of doing things. It is natural, unaffected and honest. It is limited by function, materials and manufacturing processes. Undismayed, the creative artist or designer recognizes these limitations and rises above them to produce something simple, direct, and beautiful."

Truth and Beauty

Church design is a special branch of architecture. It cannot follow the plan of secular buildings for several reasons. The church is a one-story building. It has no steel skeleton. Its interior is not divided into rooms. As it is different in purpose and structure from all other buildings it must be designed by specialists as are hospitals, schools, and theaters.

The Church is universal in thought. It emphasizes no one virtue to the exclusion of others but its edifices must have beauty of form, of external surface, and of internal structure. It may not go to extremes to attract attention but must be conservative yet ever pleasing in variety. It must represent spiritual ideas with earthly material. The house of worship is sacred. Not only must it be well built but it must have the virtues of honesty, sincerity, and humility. It must represent Christ to the world. No false pretense may enter its structure or final appearance. If commercial buildings must be honest for art's sake, the church building has a higher purpose. It must represent Divine Truth. In the past the best architecture has ever been religious. The Church may today do a service to humanity by preserving virtue in architecture. Church buildings are not the largest, highest, and richest fabrics, but may they ever be spiritually the best.

American Adaptation of Styles

Excess of ornament is tiresome in any of the arts; in painting, sculpture, literature, or music. But good taste and classical perfection, with dignified restraint, render a work in any of the arts lasting beyond all change of style and taste. Gothic is the opposite of classical, but even a Gothic church may have classical perfection. The regular irregularity of Rheims cathedral made it almost as precious as human life. And that same classical balance of reserve and abandon is a note of modern American church architecture. Our timid, experimental eclecticism finally developed into a new style. No matter whether a new church is called Gothic, Lombard, or Renaissance, it has a characteristic power of structure, with classical rhythm and balance, and only the ornamental detail is Gothic, Lombard, or Renaissance. It should be a simple matter to develop artists who can now prudently advance the rest of the way and produce designed ornament not copied from other buildings.

The number of praiseworthy edifices erected in the United States is now quite large and we shall not attempt to make a complete survey, since that is not necessary for the purpose of the present book. Those already mentioned have structural principles worth noting. Many other churches equally good in design and appearance, might have been listed. And yet, at the beginning of the twentieth century all churches were commonplace.

The late Father Durward, of Baraboo, Wisconsin, an artist and author, in the Preface to his little volume, *The Building of a Church,* caustically remarked: "If the devil were an architect

I would think that many clergymen employed him to draw their plans." That was in 1902. But now practically all new designs have some merit. Once architects did not dare to draw a single line different from at least something they had seen elsewhere. Now they display more freedom, confidence, and imagination.

The Gothic revival presented examples of church beauty and showed the need of general improvement in church design. One of the first Catholic churches in better Gothic — if a little repetition may be permitted here for the sake of order — was the Dominican Church of St. Vincent Ferrer, in New York. It has monastic simplicity combined with Gothic richness. We behold here no useless steeples or excess of ornament. Every exterior view pleases the eye. We admire the massive power of a great engineering project combined with a refined delicacy of ornament. The high, graceful nave, the warm color of tiled walls, and the soft relief of altar drapery — all help to make the interior inviting.

The design of the National Shrine of the Catholic University of Washington, by Maginnis and Walsh, is familiar to readers. In the plan, not yet an accomplished fact, we have a high nave and a high, round-arched, recessed portal, not found in ancient Lombard churches. The latter were developments of the Norman, a related style, and belonging to later Gothic churches. But majestic height is not the privilege of any one style. We are willing to learn from the past, but, as has so often been repeated, we must make our own contributions. Although a high nave was not used in every ancient style, yet once we have experienced its power we find in it an architectural feature that may be utilized in any style.

Many parish churches have been designed by Maginnis and Walsh in the Lombard style, adapted to modern conditions. The style is suited to small churches insofar as brick construction may here be used, while a rose window and an entrance porch are sufficient ornament of form. The style is equally suited to a large church as the Romanesque is capable of great majesty. The ancient churches of Lombardy themselves have been repaired in other styles, and so, too, the modern adaptations may have gathered an idea here and another there, and the new churches thus erected are not mere copies of any ancient model.

More attention is now being given to group planning. Formerly buildings were erected at various times and planned by different architects without any regard for unity. But at present an attempt is being made to match the new structures with other buildings of the parish group, and even with the secular buildings along the same street or in the general neighborhood. The habit of city planning has shown us the excellence of this custom. In Europe many great cathedrals have been placed on hilltops, or at the end of city streets, to make the church the climax of a vista of beauty. Location along a boulevard, or facing a park gives this advantage. As examples of successful grouping, we need but call attention to the Springfield, Illinois, cathedral group, in cream-colored Mankato stone, and the Mundelein Seminary, at Chicago, in the Colonial style.

The Mundelein College for Girls, in Chicago, is the first skyscraper school of modern design and is an achievement in architecture. The entrance is flanked by two gigantic angels. It is an approach which for dignity has few equals. Reference was made elsewhere to a gigantic statue of the Blessed Virgin Mary on a hospital front, in Münster, Germany. The idea is good for a church front. A large figure of Christ carved in relief on the entire height of the church would leave no doubt about the purpose of the building.

In the chapel of the Girls' College there is an interesting combination of Gothic and modern design. Gothic ornament was used to show the connection of the church with the past, but that was scarcely necessary. The altar, sanctuary lamp, and Stations

FRONT ENTRANCE, SLOVAK GIRLS' ACADEMY, DANVILLE, PA.

Harry Sternfeld, Architect, University of Pennsylvania, Philadelphia, Pa.

B. E. Starr, Associate Architect

The tower with its massive buttresses shows the rugged strength of stone. A tower must be vertical at least in outline and the most appropriate design is a perpendicular unit such as this. The broad building makes a good base for the tower which balances the plan.

of the Cross would be reminders of tradition, even if designed in a modern style. Among the many visitors to the College no one has criticized the modern style of design. Many are bitterly opposed to it in theory, but that is because they have in mind only the distortions of extremists. An artistic work in modern treatment is approved as readily as a building in any traditional style. It is a question of beauty and reverence, rather than a choice of style.

Another original school design is that of the Slovak Girls' Academy, of Danville, Pennsylvania, planned by Harry Sternfeld, architect. It cannot be classed with any ancient style, but it has beauty, spirituality, and power. Its main feature is a bell tower in which the lines are vertical. The two wings of the building with their long horizontal levels make an appropriate base. Instead of being divided into sections or stories, the illogical form of many ancient towers, this rough-hewn stone tower has four powerful buttresses terminating in a cross. Thus the tower is a single vertical unit. Each side has two parallel lines of pierced tracery with religious symbols. These and the cross are illuminated at night. Wanderers of the air are guided by it and there is the suggestion of the Church as the director of souls. This splendid building is an added proof that buildings need not be Gothic or Romanesque to have a religious atmosphere.

In the past two years the Catholic Church has taken a leading part in the development of an original but esthetic style of architecture. It was argued beforehand that any departure from tradition would not be appropriate in a church or associated building, but we are dealing now with an accomplished fact. It has been shown that buildings may be original and at the same time reverent.

May we venture a prediction? The extreme modernistic style of architecture will become more conservative here in America and by giving some attention to beauty of form will join the

REAR ENTRANCE, SLOVAK GIRLS' ACADEMY, DANVILLE, PA.

Harry Sternfeld, Architect, University of Pennsylvania, Philadelphia, Pa.

B. E. Starr, Associate Architect

This design belongs to no ancient style yet it has depth, variety and power.
It is a justification for originality.

[230]

RECEPTION ROOM UNDER THE TOWER, SLOVAK GIRLS'
ACADEMY, DANVILLE, PA.

Harry Sternfeld, Architect, University of Pennsylvania, Philadelphia, Pa.

B. E. Starr, Associate Architect

The ornament is modern but not modernistic. There is scholastic dignity
and refinement showing Catholic education adjusted to and leading contemporary design.

[231]

ENTRANCE, SS. PETER AND PAUL CHURCH, WILMINGTON, CALIF.

Henry Carlton Newton and Robert Dennis Murray, Architects, Los Angeles, Calif.

Columns and other details of precast concrete. The remainder of the building is of poured concrete, with ten-inch board forms to give right proportion to the markings. The mahogany doors are carved with symbols of Saints Peter and Paul.

conservative modern style in the planning of buildings of beauty as well as utility. Already there are signs of such capitulation. Landscaping is used to give natural beauty to the scene, and colors are being suggested by insurgents as an appeal to the esthetic sense. A recent exhibit of the "International Style" in Chicago contained color schemes by Joseph Urban for the buildings of the Chicago Exposition. Harmony of color added to beauty of form would be heresy in the International ranks but to others it would mean a return to truth. When modernistic architects change their philosophy and stop trying to be shocking, and strive to please the eye as well as satisfy the square and the plumb line, they will be on the way toward a great contribution to modern civilization. When the style recognizes spiritual values it may be used even for churches, but at present the fundamental principles are wrong and "an evil tree cannot bring forth good fruit."

Americans have given evidence that they can design a truly devotional, liturgical, and artistic church, and can plan schools with a religious atmosphere without slavish dependence on the inventiveness of architects of long-past ages. It is a strange coincidence that while America had some little part in the starting of a movement for new methods of structure and ornament, she yet wisely refused to follow the wanderings of extremists and therefore it is that many now look to this country as the stronghold of good taste. We stand on the threshold of a time of great accomplishments for the Church. God's earthly tabernacle will be an attempt at worthiness, worshipers will feel the urge to pray in a building of which the very walls are sacramentals, and unbelievers will be attracted by what to us is worship and to them is art.

NAVE, SS. PETER AND PAUL CHURCH, WILMINGTON, CALIF.

Henry Carlton Newton and Robert Dennis Murray, Architects, Los Angeles, Calif.

An example of internal arrangement of concrete walls. All of the interior is of concrete except the altar, pulpit, and Communion railing, which are of Carrara marble. Pillars and capitals are of monolithic concrete, poured in place. A well-designed sanctuary with altar as the focal point. The baldachin is of concrete. White sand was used with aggregate in four colors. The surface was carved to bring out the color harmony.

Chapter XII

STRUCTURAL QUALITIES OF MATERIAL

GREAT progress has been made in American architecture within the past few years, since more attention has been given to the nature of building material. In earlier years, when the first move in planning a church was the decision to copy a certain famous building, without consideration of the material to be used or of building conditions, there was always some lack of propriety. A stone Gothic church was copied in brick, spans were too wide and rectangular ornament inappropriate. For example, the admirer of a certain work of art, who knows nothing about painting, will, in trying to copy this work, use the wrong colors and wrong shading and the effect will be amateurish and unattractive. The would-be artist does not know his medium. And in architecture more is required than a love of the beauty of work accomplished. The builder must know his material and his tools.

This being so, it is not surprising that a great deal of the improvement in design came from those who furnish the material. At one time they recognized no obligation other than the sale of the material. A dealer in cement did not care what the buyer did with it; a dealer in stone would not care to see the building which was erected with his material. But now each group of dealers is interested in the improvement of design for their product. Modern sales efficiency has contributed as much to the advancement of art in building as have the architects. Both working together have produced remarkable results. Architects began to talk of logical structure, the suppliers of building material encouraged the scientific study of structural qualities, and finally, both groups were aided by tests made in the United States Bureau of Standards in Washington. Thus, science came to the aid of art.

Let us study each material in turn.

Stone

Concrete structure was discussed in the previous chapter. Concrete possesses more possibilities of new design for the simple reason that it has never been fully developed and because the present plan of reinforcement gives it new structural qualities. Stone structure was carried to perfection by Gothic builders and apparently is incapable of being used in any new way. But with stone side walls we can now effectively combine a concrete roof and concrete supporting arches. The arches themselves are capable of being molded into various curves to supply a great variety of interior design. Or, again, combined with straight side walls of stone, concrete pilasters can be made to support a concrete roof and the upright parallel lines will then present a classical appearance.

As an example of a church with stone walls and a concrete roof we may here consider the church of St. Philip Neri, in Chicago. The exterior shows no departure from recent Gothic designs, except in the roof, which is constructed of concrete. In the interior there is no pretense at vaulting the ceiling, although a concrete roof could readily have been elevated in that manner. But ignoring the dictates of tradition, the ceiling is built flat, with panels of color. The nave is wide and without pillars. There is a chancel choir. The walls are acoustically treated and the altar may be seen from every seat. The church is practical and liturgical, rather than traditionally artistic, and yet beauty of form has not been neglected. The point we wish to make is that it is not ancient Gothic. It is adapted to present conditions and needs.

[236]

Granite

Granite is hard and lasting in quality. It suffers no deterioration from weather. It is a proper material for churches, since they are desired to be lasting. Many of the modern churches illustrated in this book are constructed of granite. The individual church represents the Universal Church, and there is symbolism in the use of everlasting stone. Then, besides, granite is rich in color. When polished, it almost equals the beauty of precious jewels. When left seam-faced, its rough texture takes on a variety of color from the refractions of light, so that a granite wall requires little ornament except its own natural beauty.

Granite is difficult to carve, and so a functional design in granite will have little carved detail, although it must have some relief or variety in outline or a contrast in other material. In nature, we do not see a mountain of granite without some contrast in color and outline. There are high peaks, low ravines, and some discoloration as a foil to the brilliance of the predominant color. Similarly, a church built of granite should have a variety of outline and some carved ornament. Without such diversity it would be only a pile of stones. With too much ornament it would lose the spirit of granite: it would not suggest the strength, dignity, and permanence of a mountain as it came from the hand of God.

Marble

Marble has always been popular in churches but more for interior ornament than for wall structure. It is costly and not always available near the place of building. The ancient Greeks and Romans, who used so much marble, did not use it commonly for wall structure, but for pillars and the surfacing of the façade and for the ornamentation of interior walls and floors. Usually temples were small and were constructed entirely of marble. Larger buildings were of brick or concrete ornamented by marble. Some medieval churches had marble walls, especially in Italy, where marble was available. The old ivory patina of marble has an effect of dignified old age. Weather deterioration is resisted to such an extent that fine details of carving are preserved for centuries. A material of lesser worth would not deserve the careful work of artists but marble preserves the delicacy of a master stroke for succeeding ages. It was well suited for the lacelike work of Gothic cathedrals. Granite would have been less suited for carving. But modern Gothic has beauty of structure rather than of ornament and granite is quite suitable for massive masonry. Marble is best for classical whiteness and delicacy. Mankato, Minnesota, marble has a warmth of light-buff color which mellows the appearance of a wall whose outlines have the brusqueness of stone.

Limestone

Limestone has played a great part in American building. It is easily worked. Machine methods have reduced cost. It is available in large quantities. A pyramid which could be built by the ancient Egyptians only with many years of labor of a great number of slaves could be erected in one year by modern methods of quarrying, finishing, transportation, and construction. What was a tremendous feat of engineering for the Egyptians would now be but an ordinary task. And who will say that present methods are not acceptable merely because they are modern? A commercial age is not necessarily an artistic age but it may be so. One does not exclude the other. A stonecutter using modern machinery may be as great an artist as a medieval master who worked slowly by hand. Now the superficial work is done by machinery and the finishing touch is given by hand. The ancients were obliged to do a great deal of unprofitable chiseling which was only a preparation for the real work of the artist.

Limestone has a natural beauty. It is bright in color and gives a cheerful appearance to a city street. It has a variety of texture, especially if taken from various parts of a quarry. The gray suggests the strength of stone and the soft creamy tints hint of the venerability of age. Indiana limestone has the advantage of being easily worked when first quarried and it hardens with age.

Functional construction requires a stone building to have direct lines showing strength, and plain wall masses suggesting solidity. In the early post-war building boom, American buildings were erected in the pyramidal style of a pile of boxes. In a general view of a city a group of such buildings is as uninteresting as a row of shipping docks. The need of ornament was soon recognized and now it is an important part of every design. It is restricted in amount, but its requirements thus become more exacting. Limestone is easily carved, but if we are building for the ages, sharp detail must be avoided. Low relief is best suited to soft stone. Good effects have been attained by intaglio, cutting in the outlines instead of raising them in relief. A mere outline of figures is effective in several examples. Rectangular lines usually call for ornament in conventional design, so we see formal decoration confined to rectangular space. But limestone is also capable of refinement of detail, as we see in the crucifix over the entrance door of the church of St. Vincent Ferrer, in New York.

Unless there be variety of color, limestone becomes monotonous with age; hence, other material should be used for contrast. Marble, stone, brick, and terra cotta have been used for this purpose. All materials do not age in the same way, so variety of color and texture are preserved.

Functional design must recognize the purpose of a church. It may not be planned in a way similar to commercial buildings. The skyscraper style is based on steel construction and churches do not have steel framework. Church towers, being high and geometric in outline, may follow to a certain extent the prevailing style of design. It is worthy of note that square towers are more popular at present than pointed steeples. Contemporary conditions require rectangular lines. The ancient Gothic style was entirely logical for a building constructed all of stone, inclusive of the roof. Stone-roof construction was somewhat far-fetched in purpose, but once it was decided to use stone the Gothic vault and pointed arch were the natural results. In thirteenth-century churches there was perfect logic in construction and exact articulation. We hesitate to criticize the most beautiful works of all architectural history, yet, while there was logic in the distribution of weight and stress in the Gothic churches, there seems to have been faulty reasoning (at least in late Gothic) in the avoidance of every appearance of strength and weight. It was clever but unreasonable to disguise the nature of stone.

The strength of stone is vertical. Its use to span a Gothic roof was an adventure in engineering and in art. It was successful and beautiful, but it is no longer the best method, nor, because of its familiarity, is it the most interesting. Concrete roof construction may be as varied as the number of churches. In the functional design of side walls intended to support a concrete roof vertical lines should predominate, since that would be the direction of pressure and there would be but little lateral spread.

A considerable number of commercial buildings erected in recent years have followed a form of design well suited to churches. The stone façade is an arch, similar to a triumphal arch. The strength of stone is shown by the lack of ornament. Beneath the arch are the entrance, the windows and panels, richly ornamented. It is suggestive of the Transportation Building by Sullivan, at the Columbian Exposition, and may have been inspired by it.

For church design, a cross would surmount the arch and the ornamental detail would represent religious subjects. The church of St. Pascal, in Chicago, is somewhat similar to this style although the arch is not flat but pointed. Many churches designed in recent years in the Lombard style are suggestive of an arch.

The idea is appropriate as the church front should be an invitation to enter. The plan is especially good for a small church without a tower. The recessed door gives depth to the design. It is a great improvement over the flat walls of older churches. The design is aided by the omission of the cornice which once furnished variety of line and gave a slight perspective. A better perspective is provided by a deep entrance contrasted by the powerful lines of a stone arch.

Brick

Brick has its own peculiarities and calls for special design. The brick unit is small and rectangular. Therefore it cannot span a flat arch unless used with other building material and, because of its straight lines, it must be laid in geometric designs. The common brick used by our forefathers was dull as any material could well be. But now there is a great variety in color and surface of brick, and there are great possibilities for beauty of wall and variety of ornament in this diversity. Brick is a lasting material. Some of the oldest monuments of antiquity, built of brick, have fallen but have crumbled no more than stone. Brick is more lasting than concrete and has a more pleasing appearance. For that reason some concrete buildings in Europe have a surface veneer of brick. That is true of the church in Vincennes, Paris, shown on page 205. But where the brick is embedded in concrete there is danger of unequal contraction and expansion, although we have a test in concrete pavement with brick surface which has withstood the trial of time. As concrete is cast in one piece it has greater crushing strength than any other material. It is best, therefore, for arches and foundations, or wherever weight is to be supported. Other material is better for beauty and endurance. In California, due to Mission traditions, they find beauty even in the rough surface of concrete.

On account of small units the strength of a brick wall is in its resistance of vertical pressure. An arch of brick offers no great resistance to bending pressure. In England, for many years, lateral spans of brick have been reinforced with steel, in the same manner as in concrete construction. Recently, spiral stairways and other difficult constructions have been done in brick. It is a sufficiently strong but not a logical construction. An old architectural axiom requires the means of support to be visible. A hidden support for structure, which seems to be doing work beyond its strength, is poor architecture. One of the faults of some modernistic buildings is the use of slender pillars of concrete which are scientifically adequate but do not appear so to the observer. A building should not give the appearance of being in danger of collapsing. That is one reason why an architect must be more than a structural engineer. A building must not only be well supported but it must satisfy the eye. That is a reason for preference of crude brick or concrete piers over beautiful but tenuous pillars of marble. It also explains the restless spirit which comes over one in a church in which the ceiling is heavily timbered in dark wood and the side walls go unnoticed. The heavy ceiling seems to crush the spirit, even though one knows the builders have made the structure safe. But in a church in which the buttressed and recessed walls are evidently strong and lasting, what a sense of peace and repose! We enjoy kneeling in prayer at the base of a heavy pier just as, standing at the foot of a mountain, we feel a sense of confidence in God. The massive pile seems to give protection and freedom from change. It inspires a feeling of eternal peace.

But of late structural problems have become largely mathematical problems. The results of scientific tests of brick, singly and in walls, are published in two small volumes by Major L. B. Lent, issued by the Common Brick Manufacturers Association of America. Credit is hereby given to those volumes for some of the statements made here.

One of the difficulties of the continued good appearance of

brick construction is the discoloration of bricks from moisture. We are told in the volumes mentioned that this comes not from absorption of water by individual bricks, but from mortar joints which are not tight, and from faulty design and construction which do not turn water from the wall and prevent dampness.

Variety of appearance in brick walls may be attained by different bonds, by assorted colors and textures of brick, by string courses and bands, and by geometric designs. The present predominance of vertical and horizontal lines in architecture is well suited to brick construction. It is the logical use of that material.

Old brick buildings in England have a charm about them produced by studied designs. Buttresses are not exact but have broken lines. Indentations give depth of appearance to the wall. There is evidence of bricks laid lovingly by artisans who enjoyed their work. Our modern mechanical perfection is the opposite of art. An inspector would reject work which was a little imperfect but that inexactness would prove it to be not mechanical but a human effort.

Logical construction in brick is not new. The majority of churches of the past generation were usually of brick, with stone trim, and the brick walls had geometric designs, but the bricks were monotonous in color and shelled with age. These are faults which may be easily avoided in a new building.

The Richardson Romanesque style was well suited to brick construction, with stone trim, but that style was poorly handled and has lost favor. New developments, however, have taken place in the manufacture of brick which create new possibilities of design. Many colors and textures are now on the market. Contrast in colors gives a great range of geometric ornament and the rectangular shape of the bricks is a feature not to be ignored by designers. The churches of St. Thomas the Apostle, in Chicago, and of Christ the King, in Tulsa, Oklahoma, designed by Barry Byrne, are original in plan and a logical development of brick

INTERIOR OF CHAPEL, CARMELITE CONVENT OF THE INFANT
JESUS, SANTA CLARA, CALIF.

Maginnis and Walsh, Architects, Boston, Mass.

Showing the use of terra cotta for ornamental detail. A dignified and inspiring
design. The extravagant Spanish Renaissance is here placed under restraint.
Notice the crown as a canopy above the tabernacle.

and terra-cotta construction. There are vertical shafts of parallel lines attracting attention to the rectangular form of the brick unit. Cornice and pinnacles are modeled of terra cotta, which unlike brick may be irregular in form and give variety to the plan and a contrast to the rectangular lines. Window lintels could not be flat unless made of stone, so they are angular here to suit the brick construction. In his new church in Cork, Ireland, Mr. Byrne went over to the extremists.

The church of St. Thomas the Apostle is original in design and belongs to no traditional style. It is a church of great appeal in its outward appearance. The baptistry shows good taste and careful planning. Unlike other modern churches, real beauty has been achieved along with inventiveness. Critics are unfair when they express disapproval of the entire structure on account of pictures in the interior, in the modern manner. The church is a distinct achievement in design and a great contribution to the development of American church building.

Terra Cotta

Terra cotta is closely allied to brick, as it is made of clay. In ancient times it was a common medium of ornament, but has recently become popular as a structural material. In high buildings, with skeleton construction, the walls, since they have only their own weight to support, may be of light material, such as terra cotta. This has advantages of beauty, since it comes in a great variety of colors. Once it was used as an imitation of marble or granite, but the plea for honesty of material led manufacturers to consider it a lawful building material in itself and not merely an imitation of something else. It is now available in an almost unlimited number of colors and combinations of colors. Its use has made city streets much more cheerful in appearance.

Terra cotta is strong and durable. Where used in medieval Italy it has withstood weather and time. The ancient Greeks painted the exteriors of their buildings with colored wax, but it did not last. Glazed terra cotta will retain its fresh appearance for centuries. It was used in the ornamentation of the Philadelphia Museum of Art, in classical Grecian colors which will endure.

A brick or stone wall requires ornament for which terra cotta may well be used. For church ornament in that medium we have the excellent traditions of the Della Robbia family, whose artistic designs made clay more precious than marble.

A plastic material has possibilities foreign to other substances. The designer may give free reign to his fancy and plan any unusual composition of line and color. It can all be produced in terra cotta. Like other associations of dealers in building material the members of the National Terra Cotta Society are willing to aid in artistic design and to develop the logical and beautifying use of their product.

The use of color in external walls has been neglected until recently in church design. A church like the cathedral of Orvieto, Italy, with the façade covered with carved marble and a glorious display of colored mosaic, would be prohibitive in cost for most parish churches, but a church front could be done in polychrome terra cotta by artists without great expense. And, aside from consideration of economy, a wall of stone needs some contrast of color which may be supplied by even a small picture or sacred emblem. It will not detract from the solid appearance of the wall and, being small, the emblem will seem more precious. We resent the habit which writers have of referring to churches as "somber." A monastic chapel may be severely plain, but dull austerity is not a desirable quality in a parish church. Lent is but a small portion of the liturgical year.

Another important quality of terra cotta is lightness of weight. A parapet or other ornamental top of a bell tower, if made of stone, would require a heavy wall beneath to support the weight. But terra cotta, being lighter in weight, can be supported by a less massive wall.

But the large field for the use of terra cotta in churches is for interior walls and ornament. It is a superficial wall covering and is less desirable than the surface of the structural wall, but there is no imitation in the use of it. Wall tile is in such common use that it is never mistaken for structural material. As a concession to functional design it might be well to have piers, buttresses, and arches left in the natural appearance of concrete, brick, or stone and the intervening wall plated with tile. In the church of St. Vincent Ferrer the ceiling ribs are of stone and the space between is surfaced with tile.

In combination with other material, terra cotta produces admirable results. A structure of brick must be geometric in design, but terra cotta is plastic and may be molded into any shape, while it softens the sharp angles of a brick structure. Being similar materials they harmonize well. They are used together in St. Thomas the Apostle Church, shown on page 191, and in many buildings erected in recent years. Terra-cotta ornament is used also with other material, even with granite and marble. It evades the mechanical precision of machine-molded or carved material and makes a building more human and organic. It gives the architect more freedom of design and shows the human touch of the workmen.

The new use of metals should be mentioned. Chromium and aluminum are rustproof and stainproof, and are excellent for ornament as well as for permanence.

These new developments in color and texture of old material, and new methods of production and construction lead to new designs. The carving of stone on the location and under the direction of a master builder is too slow and laborious a method, when good results in substance and spirit may be attained by modern methods and materials. To save time and money, the builders of new churches in Europe used new methods, but they made too complete a break with the past. Their staggered designs are like mechanical toys. They lack beauty and harmony.

They narrowly missed greatness of achievement, because a consideration of esthetic principles would have made the new style a distinctive contribution to church architecture. But the rejection of all past principles was too great a handicap. Without harmony, unity, or beauty there remains only novelty. Importance is given to light, air, and solidity of structure. The modernists care for the body and neglect the soul.

And, strange to say, American architects at the same period began for the first time in a century to love beauty. They give proper consideration to rapidity of construction, permanence and functional design, but together with these they preserve esthetic principles which are a treasured heritage of the un-American past. The studied avoidance of those principles elsewhere is decadence. The preservation of those same principles and their use in solving new problems in American construction gives rise to a new style of architecture. We need not fear the invasion of a strange style. The choice has been made. The few buildings erected in the European style on American soil have been rejected by the man in the street and by the majority of architects and artists at once. Fads will quickly become outdated, but the well-proportioned new American style is classical in spirit and will never grow old. We do not hate the past so much as to reject fundamental principles. We like novelty and inventiveness, but we are not inclined toward anarchy. We do not demand that every building be entirely original in plan. The modernists have already begun to imitate the work of their neighbors. Only one effort can be entirely original.

We should be satisfied with a practical solution of the local problem of size and cost and the inclusion of a new painting or a new design of entrance, even though the remainder of the building be much like other structures. Originality is important but not so much so that tradition, beauty, and reverence must be sacrificed for its sake. We may use new metals, cover the ceiling with sound-absorbing material, and construct walls by such new methods as the assembling of sections of precast concrete. In so doing, the old "styles" will be abandoned. The ancients built in a way which was natural for them. If we do the same, our buildings will be different from anything done before. A good building is not necessarily a copy of an old building accepted by all as a model of excellence. "A good building is the product of a good architect, a good contractor, and good craftsmen using good materials." Real artists will not allow themselves to be limited by a "style." They will build in a natural way and the high quality of the result will be seen in the excellence of every surface and line.

At least in church construction, the material is of secondary importance, although influencing the design. Efficient construction is valuable but submissive to the spirit of reverence. The ground plan of a church may depart but little from tradition. There may be no change in the location of the main altar, the Communion railing, baptismal font and sacristies. Side altars are not so fixed in position. American custom has placed altars at the end of each side aisle, but there is no rule requiring them to be so placed. They may be omitted, or placed in niches along the side walls, or in the transepts. Statues of saints on pedestals or in niches may take the place of side altars.

Tradition requires Stations of the Cross and religious pictures, in which no great deviation of style is allowable, but they may be painted or carved in a contemporary style, provided it is reverential. The subject of the picture is of more importance than the style of the artist. If the style interferes with the proper presentation of the subject, it is not good religious art.

Beyond the requirements of tradition, as outlined in the foregoing, the walls and roof may be constructed in any desired manner, so long as they convey the spirit of reverence. That is the final test of all church art and architecture. It was once thought that reverence could be suggested only by a building in a familiar ancient style. That was the easiest way, as it required no inventiveness. It is still the best way for a second-rate architect. If his design be inferior, it will at least suggest something better. A few imitative weather-stains and supposed wormholes bored in the woodwork to give an antique effect will remind the beholder that there were great artists in medieval times if not now. A better designer will not be satisfied to praise the devotion of a past age. He will remind the worshiper that in spite of the faults of the present age even now reverence for the House of God may be shown by creative effort.

Chapter XIII

SOME FINAL CONCLUSIONS

TO sum up, then, we must improve our church designing, and especially its furnishing and decorating. But the bizarre, the primitive, the distorted and decadent are not for us. Only the dignified, solid, honest, and beautiful can represent the ancient Church. We must regain the lost love of the fine arts as an aid to devotion, and must not allow ourselves to fall into complete oblivion in regard to the past. We are not so much in want of a better style as of better taste.

From time to time the need of Catholic art schools is urged. A school consists of an instructor and a few seats, or in this case, a workshop. The difficulty is not in the erection of a building, but in the finding of instructors. A school which would teach students to make copies of works of art of one favorite style would do more harm than good. If recognized as a leader, it would delay progress in church design for many years. We can copy from the past without the aid of schools. Work of the mind is needed rather than of the hand. Although skillful hands have produced many great works of art, all progress in design came from the minds of thinkers. The generals in the rear planned the advance of each unit. It is easy to develop trained artisans, but the very beginning of progress is in correct thinking about art and architecture.

What is needed, therefore, is a school in which students, after learning the technique of the past, would be encouraged to create original designs under the supervision of an architect, with definite ideas for the betterment of church design. That was the plan of the medieval guilds. Individuals had considerable liberty for inventions, but the general plan was drawn by the master builder.

[251]

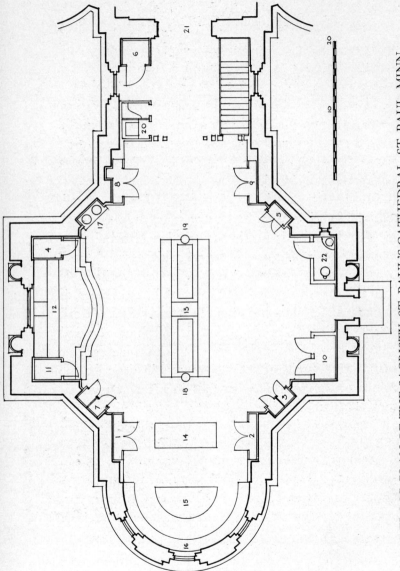

FLOOR PLAN OF THE SACRISTY, ST. PAUL'S CATHEDRAL, ST. PAUL, MINN.

Maginnis and Walsh, Architects, Boston, Mass.

A cathedral sacristy must provide for a greater number of clergy than the sacristy of a
parish church. The arrangement here is complete.

1, 2, 3, 4, 5, 6, closets; 7, linen closet; 8, 9, cases for albs; 10, coat closet; 11, safe; 12, archbishop's
vestment case; 13, vestment case; 14, table; 15, case for copes; 16, seat; 17, sacrarium; 18, 19, lavabo;
20, confessional; 21, entrance to Cathedral; 22, washroom.

INTERIOR OF SACRISTY, ST. PAUL'S CATHEDRAL,
ST. PAUL, MINN.

Maginnis and Walsh, Architects, Boston, Mass.

Attractive appearance of a convenient sacristy. In harmony with the Italian
Renaissance style of the rest of the church.

[253]

CHURCH ARCHITECTURE

In all good church design everything is subservient to architecture. In violation of this first principle, decorators ignore the outline of the interior and paint in bright colors wherever they please, drawing attention away from walls, pillars, and roof. Pictures are introduced in tints which do not harmonize with colors elsewhere in the church, and in which curved lines break up the lines of the wall. Windows are introduced which by their brightness and wrong color effects clash with everything in the church. It may be possible to admire the windows by themselves or the building by itself, but to enjoy both together is an impossibility. Altars, again, are designed as pictures rather than as structures. They have no depth and usually do not harmonize with the design or colors of the interior. White altars have a symbolism of spirituality, but the rest of the church is then supposed to lead up to that spirituality. The altars should not stand apart. Further, there is too much dainty prettiness in our altars. Highly polished white marble, draped with spiderweb lace, does not represent an everlasting Church. Good ladies, in charge of the sanctuary, may hang a beautiful but flimsy lace at the foot of a massive statue, thus breaking the continuity between the solid base and its weighty statue. The statue itself is thus completely taken out of its relation to the general design. These few illustrations may help to impress the great fact which we must never allow ourselves to forget, that furniture, ornaments, and painted decoration must all be considered integral parts of the church design.

Like the altars, many façades lack depth. They are treated as flat walls rather than articulate parts of the buildings which they front. Ancient churches had depth from the very character of their structure. The stone walls were thick and hence every opening for window or door was deeply set. Richly carved, deep portals were prominent features of the great cathedrals. But walls now are thin and the depth of entrance portal can be attained only by a porch or entrance hall. It is easily planned but often neglected.

The façade should be an essential part of the church plan and not a false front. Italian Baroque churches have a west front higher than the nave, and bearing only an accidental connection with the rest of the church. Some Gothic façades also, are independent of the general plan of the church. That was rare in Gothic design. Medieval designers strove for structural logic. The modern demand for an articulated plan requires that the front be not a separate, showy entity, but an organic part of the church. In the new Westminster Cathedral the façade begins to recede, step by step, a little above the entrance portal. Thus the front harmonizes with the sides in outline, while interest is centered in the bell tower.

We are often told of the importance of hiring a good architect but the question arises, "Who is good?" One who has been popular and designed many churches is not necessarily a worthy designer. Good church planning is something entirely new. It is not taught by art schools. It comes by inspiration and cannot be learned or copied.

Calling for competitive plans is not the best method of awarding work. The best architects are unwilling to devote time to sketches which may be rejected. A rough sketch might easily be the best one presented and be rejected in favor of a beautiful work of art showing trees, clouds, and passing autos. A building committee usually selects what is common and familiar. The surface texture of brick or stone is not exactly represented in a plan and must be imagined. The sketch cannot show the final appearance and it would be a mistake to assign work on the merits of an imaginary front elevation without consideration for the inner arrangement. If several architects are desired as competitors, they should be paid for their plans as a matter of justice and to secure best efforts.

[255]

To speak of hiring the best architect gives no aid. Everyone wishes the best but many have no standards by which to judge. But an architect may be judged by his previous work. This will show what style he favors or whether he is independent and original. If he has worked in an old style, notice should be taken whether it was treated in an understanding way and adapted to present conditions. Even a style which was originally ornate should be treated now with reserve and simplicity. Those addicted to modernistic distortions are not capable of designing a church. Their way of thinking is wrong. And, on the other hand, the unqualified use of an old style is a handicap. An unusually good singer may please an audience with an old song but an ordinary singer would fail. Likewise with churches; a great architect might use worthily an old style but a lesser artist, even though he worked in marble, would produce something cheap and second-rate.

Better than a drawing in two dimensions is a clay model which has depth and shows light, shadow, and comparative masses, and might also include old buildings which are to be matched.

If other buildings are to be erected later, it is well to have one architect draw the plans for the entire group and arrange the ground plan. Even if, ten years or more later, another architect may find it necessary to make minor changes, there will be more unity in a plan drawn by one designer. Failure to thus provide for the future has made many parish groups inharmonious and crowded into a small space, or scattered on several blocks.

The architect should not ask for absolute authority of design. In recent times no architect has proved himself to be worthy of such uncritical confidence. There is need of conferences on local needs and building conditions, the preferences of pastor and people, and questions of liturgy must be decided by authorities in that science. Truly great leaders are willing to learn something from others.

At one time church spires extended above every city showing

MAIN FAÇADE, ST. ANNE'S CHURCH, SAN FRANCISCO, CALIF.

Will D. Shea, Architect, San Francisco, Calif.

This concrete church has a steel frame to prevent possible damage from earthquakes. All except the frieze is of poured concrete, showing adaptability to ornamentation.

the importance of spiritual things. Now that is impossible. The church has a better right to vertical lines, but when they have been used first by office buildings the church in the neighborhood must be harmonious in plan to a sufficient extent to fit into the picture, yet the plan should be different enough to show the superior purpose of the church. God's message is for wealth and commerce as well as for poverty and humility. Churches may be located wherever humanity needs them, but there should be a difference not only of outline but of spirit. Old churches among the high buildings of New York City are able to preserve their religious identity and their right to existence.

Where vertical lines have been used in higher buildings a church with that motif would appear subservient. There are possibilities of church design in parallel horizontal lines with a flat roof. Heretofore this plan has been used only in chapels, basements, and combination churches. In such cases it is only a temporary arrangement. But it seems possible to find in this plan something excellent in itself. On the interior, this form would provide good acoustics, and parallel lines would direct attention to the altar and suggest God's grace flowing back to the people.

Commercialism does not prevent progress in the building arts. The great ages of Gothic and Renaissance art were commercial ages, but not exclusively so. The former age was also spiritual. Americans of great wealth and no character do not correctly represent America. Some wealth is necessary for great building projects, but not great wealth. Costly churches and monasteries in Europe have always been a temptation to confiscation by unfriendly governments. What we write here of church improvement does not refer to gold and jeweled vessels and to marble walls, but to well-planned churches, even if they be of such humble material as concrete. Churches not well planned, but costly, are a waste of money.

A commercial spirit doubtless exists today, but it is not universal. There is a tendency to assume that a bank must be safe because located in a splendid edifice and that a million-dollar school building must of necessity house a perfect educational institution. There is danger, likewise, on the part of church builders that they fall into the custom of putting on a false front and

STEEL FRAME, ST. ANNE'S CHURCH, SAN FRANCISCO, CALIF.

W. Adrian, Structural Engineer

This is the first Catholic church in America to be supported entirely by a steel frame. The purpose is to prevent any possible damage of the concrete from earthquakes. The main façade, illustrated on page 257, shows how the building has been developed in concrete.

[259]

of building in a more costly way than can be justified by the purpose and the means of the people.

A parish church need not have the grandeur of a cathedral. Logical construction includes appropriateness to the location. Extravagance, on the other hand, is unworthy of a Church which teaches self-denial, while Epicureanism, the mere indulgence in the pleasure of the senses, is the very opposite of Christian austerity. The Liturgical Movement does not require glorious pageantry, which we have always had, but pastoral simplicity. Its true spirit may be perfectly observed in the small plain churches as well as beneath the loftiest cathedral arches. Let us build to worship in spirit and in truth.

INDEX

INDEX

INDEX

INDEX

INDEX

artists, 171; in German churches, 202; in old churches, 176; increase in, 226; lack of, 165, 166, 176; need of, 168; not all-important, 248; possibilities of, 213; record of, 180

Ornament, all-important in Renaissance, 87; applied, not true Gothic, 70; before structure in the Renaissance, 85; contrast of, and plain walls, 13; crude in Romanesque churches, 55; excess of, 99, 225; painted, in Romanesque churches, 55; unnecessary, 198; used sparingly, 163

Orvieto, Italy, Cathedral in colors, 246

Outline, architectural, 96

Overbeck and architectural decoration, 159

Pagan revival in Renaissance, 83

Pagan symbols used by Christians, 16

Paganism, 166, 168; and the Renaissance, 83, 90; revival of, 7

Painting, as altar piece, 120, 153; as creative art, 121

Parthenon, improving on the, 177; originally, polychromed, 190

Patmore, Coventry, quoted, xi

Pavia, Certosa of, 53

Petrarch, father of the Renaissance, 83

Philadelphia Museum of Art, 246

Pictures, religious, in non-Catholic churches, 10

Pillars, 121; add to beauty of design, 29; clustered, 67; false, in Baroque style, 92

Pius X and reform, 2

Plans, payment for, 255

Pointed arch, 67

Polychrome decoration by Greeks, 190

Prague, concrete church in, 204

Precious Blood Church, Los Angeles, 212

Proportion in Greek buildings, 163

Protestant, Colonial style not, 113

Pugins and Gothic revival, 9

Raphael, artist, 85, 90

Ravenna, 1

Realism, 87

Realists and idealists, 171

Reality in modern architecture, 174

Rebellion in Baroque style, 96

Religious atmosphere in modern building, 229

Religious spirit, 204; of Gothic churches, 8

Renaissance, 166; in America, 92, 95; in France and England, 92

Renaissance decoration, 152

Renwick, James, architect, 79

Reredos, a form of canopy, 123; high, improper, 119, 120; in St. Mark's, Venice, 119; in various styles, 119; origin of, 118

Reverence, 196; of Fra Angelico, 172; shown unconsciously, 200; spirit of, 249, 250

Revivals of old styles, 167

Rheims Cathedral, 225; an example of logical plan, 71

Ribbed vaulting, 49, 51

Ribs in Romanesque vaulting, 66

Richardson, architect, 95, 148, 169

Roman ornament versus Gothic, 143

Romanesque, American, interiors incorrect, 59; American revival of, 58; not Roman, 59; Richardsonian, 182; suitable to brick construction, 61

Romanesque decoration, 148

Romanesque revival, 169

Romanesque style, origin of, 47; suited to brick construction, 243

Rome, all styles connected with, 101

Roof construction, 74; Lamella trussless, 204

Roofs, concrete on German churches, 82; flat, less costly, 134

Rosary College, 82

Round and octagonal churches, 10, 28

Round arch, 51

Round-arch Gothic, 49

Ruskin, 161, 164, 195; preferred plain walls, 150

Sacramental Presence, 6

Sacristy, entrance to, 14

St. Ambrose Church of Milan, 53

St. Anselm's Church, New York, 162

St. Apollinare in Classe, basilica of, 25

St. Augustine, Florida, cathedral of, 113

St. Benedict College, 82

St. Cecilia, basilica of, 25, 109

St. Denis, Paris, church of, 208

St. Francis of Assisi, 142; church of, 85

St. Henry's Church, Bamberg, 204

St. Joseph's Church, Seattle, Washington, 211

St. Louis Cathedral, 42

INDEX